Me, my best self and I

Discover what you really want and how to get it

Moritz Ostwald

Copyright © 2014 by Moritz Ostwald

All rights reserved. This book or any portion thereof may not be reproduced or used in any manner whatsoever without the express written permission of the publisher except for the use of brief quotations in a book review.

Bibliographic information published by the Deutsche Nationalbibliothek

The Deutsche Nationalbibliothek lists this publication in the Deutsche Nationalbibliografie; detailed bibliographic data are available on the Internet at http://dnb.dnb.de.

First Printing, 2014

ISBN 978-1501099663

Montgolfier-Allee 19
60486 Frankfurt
Germany

www.alphacoaching.co

This book is dedicated to my wonderful wife Tanja and to my newborn, Julie Anne, and to the many, many clients and coachees from whom I learned what my real purpose is.

About the author

MORITZ IS PASSIONATE ABOUT AUTHENTIC communication, enlightened leadership and empowering people.

These passions led Moritz to co-found a mobile learning organization and a software company in Toronto.

He is the Founder and CEO of Alpha Coaching & Solutions and serves as a Peak Performance Coach focusing on Executive Coaching and Training.

He became an expert in positive psychology with one goal in mind:

"How can we empower people to live an extraordinary life and reach their full potential?"

Moritz also has extensive experience in the corporate world where, until 2010, he held various senior management positions in some of the world's leading financial institutions, including Deutsche Bank and The Bank of New York Mellon. He holds a MA in Economics and is a certified Life-Coach.

Find out more about Moritz and how he helps people to transform their lives at www.alphacoaching.co.

Moritz Ostwald

Table of Contents

Preface ix
Introduction xv
    Why this book? xv
    How to get the most out of this book xviii
1. WHO are you and WHY this is important 1
    Your Identity 2
    Your Values 7
    Your Beliefs 35
    Your Desires 52
2. WHAT do you really, really want to achieve in your life? ... 57
    Something to think about 57
    Needs vs Wants 61
3. The science of effective goal setting 65
    What are goals anyway? 65
    The importance of clear goals 70
    How to Set Effective Goals 76
4. The art of goal achieving 97
    Elegant strategies 97
    The systematic approach 128
5. NOW is a good time to take actions 141
    Where do you start? 142
    Enjoy the ride 154
6. Summary and conclusion 161
    Wrap-Up 161
    Key Learnings and feed forward 163

Preface

> "Figure out who you are and then do it on purpose."
> — Dolly Parton

The story of me learning English

IT WAS A DULL, RAINY morning one day in 1993 when Mr. Blankenburg asked the same question he asked 3 times a week: "Who would like to present their homework?"

Many arms around me went up, signaling to him that they were ready and happy to share their prepared work. All of my fellow students except Steven, Hendrik and me. We didn't do the homework.

The question was whether this time Mr. Blankenburg would pick one of the well-prepared students to stand up and speak to the whole class. Or whether he'd ask one of us 3 to deliver the homework or at the minimum: say something half meaningful.

This morning, he hesitated and waited 10 seconds, which felt like an eternity to me. I realized that today, he decided "to encourage" one of us. So I had a 2 out 3 chance that he wouldn't pick me. And just like in real life, sometimes, even if the odds look pretty good you can still lose.

"Moritz: What have you researched?"

I was in panic, my pulse raised to 170, my face turned red, I started sweating, knowing that the whole class was now waiting for me to stand up and speak. Some of my fellow students started whispering and laughing. They knew what I knew, and what my teacher also knew. I hadn't prepared the homework. Not because I didn't want to. But because I was so terrified of this exact situation that I couldn't do it.

It wasn't about a fear of speaking in public or just this class of students. The course was the foreign language "English" and I considered myself so bad at this subject that I couldn't even say one simple, straight sentence without feeling an enormous amount of worry that I would make all kinds of mistakes and humiliate myself. I felt ashamed thinking of all these embarrassing moments before, when my teacher and my fellow students expected something from me and I just did not deliver.

Mr. Blankenburg was a kind and calm gentleman who always saw the best in his students. To his surprise he just couldn't motivate me to literally step up and speak up in his English courses and overcome my fears of making mistakes and the feeling of not being good enough for the average level of this class.

He wasn't only my English teacher though. The second subject he taught me, with very different results was "Economics and Politics".

In hindsight it is very interesting to analyze what happened in my early life. The same teacher with similar passion in both topics, English and Economics, tried to teach me both subjects at the same time. I even think it's fair to say that he liked me.

So if you look at all the variables that explain why I was the best student in Economics, but the worst in English, it really only comes down to my motivation and strategies at that time. I was very interested in all kinds of economic theories and current economic events at that time, so my motivation to learn and excel in this topic was huge. Without knowing it then, I formulated a very clear outcome of what exactly I wanted to achieve (High grades) and also how I'd achieve it, by involving myself in all discussions, preparing myself for all sessions thoroughly, and not being afraid if my teacher or other students argued with my opinions (which they loved to do, altogether).

Mr. Blankenburg was far more than "just" a teacher for me: he became my first mentor who treated me with respect and was curious about my thoughts on the world. At age 16, this was a new experience for me.

And up until today, we occasionally meet with the other students of the "Economics class of 1997" in his home in Hamburg to debate and philosophize about current events and remember the good old times.

English and economy

In contrast to my high motivation in Economics, I didn't see the necessity to learn English. I had a weak start and did not have the right strategies to motivate myself, to see the big picture and to understand why it was so important to learn foreign languages. Or maybe I developed these beliefs to protect myself: "Really, who needs to speak English anyway?"

More than 20 years later, my interest in Economics is stronger than ever, so you might argue that this was foreseeable and no big surprise. What really wasn't foreseeable at all was my sudden eureka moment in the summer of 1998 shortly before I started my corporate career as an apprentice at Deutsche Bank. I realized that without a strong command of the English language, I wouldn't have a chance to become as successful as I imagined I could be.

And even in a corporation that bears "Deutsche" (which translates to "German") in their name, it became clear that they were a global business with close to 100,000 employees across the world. And I soon learned that the official language wasn't German… but of course English.

Fast forward a couple of years and a dozen private English courses and intense training sessions, I became more and more comfortable speaking and writing in English. I lost my fear in it and since then never again had the urge to be perfect in any important topic. Realizing that I was enough, it dawned on me that my English skills were also enough to make the next move. So I eventually became Global Head of Sales & Marketing for institutional banking clients and I was communicating daily with clients from around the world… in English.

And I always knew that I wasn't perfect in using this foreign language; it just didn't bother me any longer once I understood that I didn't need to be perfect.

I'm still far from being a Master of this language, but I trust it is "good enough" to express my experiences and lessons learned, my insights and new ideas, my passion for all things about the science and art of achieving our dreams and outcomes and most of all: becoming our best self!

Due to the many lessons I learned about motivation, clear outcomes and achieving goals from just this one episode, I decided to not simply hire a ghostwriter to help me manifest my outcome of writing this book. No, I decided to write it myself. In ordinary English. I'd therefore ask for your understanding for any grammatical mistakes I make. I hope that they are not bothering you too much and that you can easily follow and focus on the content.

The same blueprint that started to become clearer and clearer to me on how to achieve my outcome of learning proper English also helped in various other topics which I was reluctant about before. I literally stood and spoke up wherever I had the opportunity: I joined Toastmasters International and became "Distinguished Toastmaster," and after seven years I had given about 100 speeches and presentations… all in English. I had the opportunity to lead teams with highly talented employees early in my career. Starting from scratch, making all kinds of mistakes, but consistently improving and willing to learn. These experiences sparked my interest in Leadership and the enormous power outstanding and honest leaders have.

So it might not be a surprise either, that those 3 topics of Communication, Leadership and Peak Performance have become my core focus that I now dedicate all my time to, ever since I left the banking industry in 2010.

My wish for you is that you allow yourself to read this book with a fresh mindset of curiosity and interest in exploring new ways of thinking and acting on your very own important aspects of your life.

Let me invite you on a journey to your own feelings, to the real you, to who you are destined to be(come).

Imperfect and honest greetings from Frankfurt,

Moritz
Frankfurt, Germany
November, 10th 2014

Introduction

Why this book?

> "There's a difference between knowing the path and walking the path."
> — Morpheus - The Matrix

NOW WHY WOULD I WANT to write a book about achieving goals, when a quick search on Amazon reveals that there are more than 14,800 books on goals available? I certainly haven't read all of them, but I have read hundreds of them, been to dozens of seminars, and spent thousands upon thousands of dollars on my education. Above all, I have dedicated the last 15 years of my career to answering two questions:

How can I achieve and enjoy living a meaningful and happy life?

And how can I inspire and empower others to do the same?

One of the things that has helped me most in achieving my dream life has been to master the art and science of setting the right outcomes for the right reasons, and then achieving them. The overwhelmingly positive feedback I receive from my coaching and seminar clients encourages me to go further, every single day, step by step.

One step towards achieving my own mission is to write this book that will explain all of the vital aspects necessary to master that skill. In the process of writing, I have identified three main outcomes that this book strives to accomplish:

- It aims to show how knowing WHO you are, the reasons WHY things matter to you and your ability to achieve WHAT is really important in your life, help you become your best self.
- It aims to present a holistic view on all important aspects of goal setting and achieving.
- It aims to include many hands-on exercises that enable you, the reader, to train yourself in techniques that will help you understand what your very own personality has to do with how well you achieve your goals.

I presume that most of you have read a book or two or have been to a seminar regarding goals. Perhaps they even promised you "golden" tips on how to succeed in your life. It's as if you were going to the latest guru who prescribes 3 magic blue pills and promises your life will change dramatically.

So let me ask you: Does it?

Though I cannot guarantee that reading this book alone will transcend you to the next level, you will certainly gain a much better, holistic understanding about the factors that influence you and your likelihood of achieving your outcomes.

However, what ultimately will determine your success in becoming your best self is the daily training of your muscles both physically and mentally. You won't increase your chance of achieving more by reading or consuming any kind of text, audio, video or seminar. You will do so by getting active, performing the exercises, and applying the knowledge and best practices that you learn from this book. How often? Daily! With every important goal that really matters to you!

This way you can transform the new and difficult-looking task of applying several rules for every goal into an automated habit. How many hours did you practice driving a car, before you could handle it safely? Wasn't it the hardest task in the world to simultaneously concentrate on all the new instruments, on what was happening on the street and on what your instructor was telling you?

Now you barely think of any of these tasks consciously and I bet you are safely driving your car, right?

Why is that? Because it became a habit. It became an automated procedure which your subconscious mind is performing with ease. But of course, only after you spent a significant amount of time, energy and focus to master that skill.

I'm inviting you now to go on a similar, even more exciting journey where you will discover what you really want and learn how to master your goal setting and achieving skills! Become the go-to guy, who other people admire for your ability to follow through on the right goals, your right goals!

As much as we will dive deep into strategies on how you can achieve certain outcomes in your life, and as much as I am passionate about sharing some very powerful techniques with you within this book, let me also be perfectly clear on a strong belief I have gained over the past years:

The purpose of achieving a goal is NOT achieving this goal. The purpose is to get one step closer to your real purpose, the WHY in your life. After all, even if you achieve all the goals you can imagine and you are highly efficient in doing so, it most likely won't fulfill you and give you meaning in your life unless you know WHY any chosen goal is helping you in your personal mission.

On the deepest, most fundamental level we will come to the ultimate question you can ask yourself: Who am I? Who do I want to become? And why?

With this bigger picture in mind, let's get started.

How to get the most out of this book

> "I have no special talent. I am only passionately curious."
> — Albert Einstein

WE ARE ALL CONSTANTLY LOOKING for answers. Searching for quick fixes and the next big thing. We want to believe in the myriads of "How-to" Self-Help guides that promise us great results, almost effortlessly and in no time.

But how often have you succeeded with this approach? If how-to books actually did work, humanity wouldn't suffer that much anymore!

Maybe you also think that it is time to dig deeper, to broaden your understanding?

Maybe it is time to step up and reclaim your POWER to live the life you deserve instead of relying on gurus, authors, coaches etc. to "fix" your problems, tell you what to believe, what to do and how to live "the good life".

Maybe you don't need to be "fixed" at all! Maybe you just need a fresh, integral approach to solve your challenges yourself.

Maybe it is time to ask the right questions instead of expecting THE one right answer that'll fix all your problems.

Just imagine: What if you focus your energy and attention on working with this book and exploring YOUR answers on these 4 questions:

1. Who are YOU? Who are YOU being your best self?
2. What do YOU really want to achieve in your life?
3. Why is this YOUR ultimate outcome?
4. How will YOU achieve it?

Welcome to this different approach. The book is structured into 3 sections. In the first 2 chapters you will discover the answers to your Who, What and Why questions, empowering you with lots of distinctions, ideas and exercises. Chapter 3 and 4 will bring you up to speed with the science and art of goal setting and achieving.

Then and only then, you should move on to chapter 5 and "Get it!". Get what you deserve, what you dream of, what you desire.

Let me suggest one more thing before you start. It is in the psyche of us human beings that we tend to only notice what fits in our current model of the world.

Let's say I'm shopping for a new car. I might read a lot of newspapers and consumer reports, talk to friends, go to car dealers and build my opinion of which model is the best fit for me. Once I intellectually make my decision, something interesting happens: Because I already made up my mind, I now only focus on information that supports my decision. I start to filter all those bits which might suggest that another car is even better suited. I start to ignore warnings or negative comments from friends or the media. This often happens unconsciously and is very common behavior.

Why? We call this phenomenon "Avoiding Cognitive Dissonance". We want to feel good about our decision, we want to believe that our decision is right. So we try to avoid all doubts, negative information etc. that make us feel bad about our decision.

When I finally bought that new car, the very next day I "suddenly" began to see a lot more of the same model and even color driving around. Coincidence? And isn't this great reassurance that gives us a lot of pleasure, seeing other people with the very same excellent taste?

The same principle is true for many areas of our lives, particularly when we process new information such as reading a new book like this one.

Our brain has powerful filters that delete, distort and generalize information before we even become consciously aware of it. Practically this means that we are often only absorbing "new" information if our brain lets it through, or in other words: if it fit into our model of the world.

Being aware of this fact, there is one elegant technique to temporarily overcome this important feature of our brain. It's called the "Beginner's Mind" and was first practiced by ZEN-Buddhists. It is a very simple and easy to understand behavior. You simply ask yourself: What if I had never before seen, heard, felt, tasted or smelled this? What if I were a child and this were my very first book on the subject of becoming my best self?

To ensure maximum learning and pleasurable experience working with this book, I'd like to invite you to put yourself in such a state of the beginner's mind. And it is a very simple and fun state of consciousness, too. Before you start wondering: It's OK to enjoy yourself, have fun, explore new things and feel the joy associated with them.

Just explore with lots of curiosity and desire, what you can learn here today. Take a lot of notes, write down what you think and feel, perform every single exercise as if you'd never seen anything like it before. Make it a challenge to come up with new answers, fresh perspectives and bold ideas. In such a state of being open minded and full of curiosity, you can then very easily think of which of these new findings you'd like to convert into new, powerful habits.

In fact, I recommend that you deliberately put yourself into the beginner's mind every day. Next time you walk to your office or through a park: What can you notice that you have never seen or heard before? You'll be surprised about the many new distinctions you can make!

> "In the beginner's mind there are many possibilities, but in the expert's there are few."
> — Zen Master Shunryo Suzuki

1
WHO are you and WHY this is important

SUCCESSFUL AND FULFILLED PEOPLE NOT only know exactly what they want to accomplish in their lives and their reasons why: they also know exactly WHO they are. Not only that, they start with WHO. They understand the positive correlation between who they are, what they truly need to accomplish in their lives and why. They know how their identity, their core values and beliefs heavily influence whether or not they follow through on their outcomes. They also know that on their journey unexpected obstacles and challenges will show up which stand in the way of their goals. They know when it's wise to invest their energy in overcoming those obstacles by changing their approach; and when it's better to let go of a previous goal and concentrate on a different one.

Would you like to consider yourself as truly successful and fulfilled at the same time and living a happy and meaningful life? And are you willing to dive deep into your own psyche, challenge your current model of the world and learn new distinctions about who you are and who you need to become to achieve your very own "WHATs"? Then this chapter is for you.

If you want to become a grandmaster of your life: Always start with the WHO. Then find the WHYs for the most important WHATs in your life and finally: Get ready to rumble and be your best self!

> "People don't buy what you do; they buy why you do it. And what you do simply proves what you believe"
> — Simon Sinek

Your Identity

> "We know what we are, but know not what we may be."
> — William Shakespeare

Dependency to Values and Beliefs

UNDERSTANDING EXACTLY HOW TO SET goals is a very powerful skill that, once mastered, will set you apart from 97% of the people who just don't know, don't understand or don't follow through on these rules that have been proven to result in success.

The good news is, that you and anybody else can learn these techniques and make them a habit that massively increases your likelihood of achieving your goals. And the more you practice these skills, the more efficient you will become. Understanding the science of goal setting is critical to your ultimate success, and this book will give you the tools and techniques you need to master these skills.

Now imagine that you have already claimed for yourself the title "Master of Science in Goal Achieving"! Wow, you truly achieve all your goals and your friends admire you for these skills. You are highly efficient and no matter what, you follow through to achieve your goals.

How does it feel? Fantastic, doesn't it?

But wait: How do you know if you have pursued the "right" goals? I mean, you have achieved them, but maybe they weren't that important to you? Or you find out that there are other much more important goals in your life? This question brings us to another dimension of achieving goals. What if you were crystal clear about the importance of every single one of your goals? What if you only achieved 50% of your previous goals, but each one really mattered to you? What if you are not only efficient in your approach to achieving your goals, but effective as well? What if you are doing the "right things" while at the same time you are doing "things right"?

I'd like to call this the "WHY-Dimension".

- Why are you setting specific goals and not others?
- Why are you successfully achieving some of your goals, but failing with others?
- Why do so many people fail on their New Year's resolutions?
- Why are other people incredibly successful in the things they do? One of my teachers, Tony Robbins, has a good answer to this when he says: *"Reasons come first. Answers come second."*

Since the answers to those Why questions heavily differ from person to person, I will refer to these Why-dimension questions as the "Art of Goal setting and achieving." Before we think about which goal or task we want to work on, we should make it our first habit to ask WHY. Why is this goal worthy of your effort to achieve? One of the answers should be: "Because it supports who I am." Or "Because it helps me becoming my best self."

This chapter deals with the different aspects on the WHY. By following the exercises, you will gain a much clearer picture of who you are and what really matters to you. And once you have mastered this art, you can then apply the How-To approaches from the next section of this book to really experience breakthroughs in effective AND efficient goal setting and achieving.

Introduction to the Neurological Levels

> "Make your life a mission-not an intermission."
> — Arnold H. Glasgow

UNDERSTANDING THE CONNECTION BETWEEN WHAT we want to accomplish, why this is important and how we can achieve it is the key for a successful, holistic approach. A great model to gain a better understanding of this connection is the "Neurological levels" originally formulated by Robert Dilts in 1990.

This model serves as an excellent tool for gathering information about who you are and who you might need to become to congruently live the life you deserve.

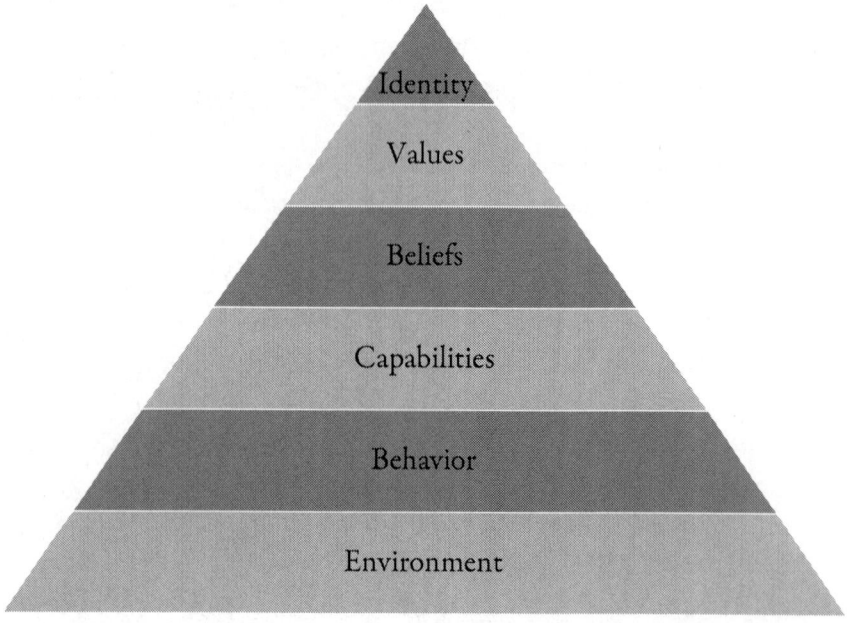

The highest 3 levels of this pyramid help us to understand WHO we are, and WHY.

Our identity is who we are.

- What is our purpose in life?
- Our mission?
- Why do we live exactly like we do?

Our core values also lead us to a better understanding of who we are.

- What do we value most in our lives?
- What are our towards-to values?
- What are our away from values?

The same is true for our limiting and empowering beliefs.

- What do we believe in?
- Which beliefs empower us?
- Which beliefs limit us in achieving our desires and goals?

Neurological Level	Eliciting question	
Spirituality	Larger Purpose	
Identity	Own Purpose: Who am I?	I, I am
Values	Why?	Own core values
Beliefs	Why?	It is, I know
Capabilities / Skills	What?	Can, Could
Behavior	How?	Do, Did
Environment	Where, When?	This, here, there

Often, people realize that they show certain behaviors that don't seem to fit with their other levels, such as their values. Something just doesn't feel right but it is often difficult to determine what exactly caused that feeling. And this is particularly true for pursuing certain goals. We cognitively try our best to achieve a goal, but if we feel something is wrong, we often sabotage reaching this goal without even realizing it. The reason for this common behavior is often a misalignment of these neurological levels, i.e., a certain goal (on the behavior level) is contradicting one or more of our important values.

An important second step after identifying and becoming aware of these is to realign these levels, so that they support each other. People who live "in line" often experience a very balanced, fulfilled life. They make decisions that are consciously aligned with their identity, values, beliefs and skills.

Therefore it is worth exploring our neurological levels in greater detail and asking ourselves: Are my goals supporting who I am, what I value and believe?

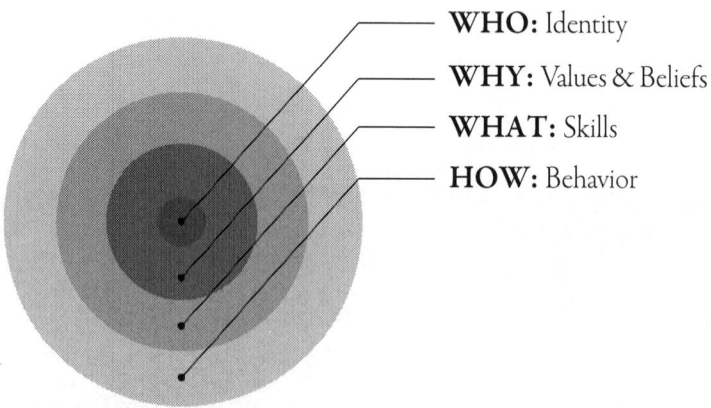

The more you understand who you are and why — your identity, your values and beliefs, your capabilities and skills — the better you can explain your behavior and the better you can set goals that are really important to you. And by aligning your goals with your neurological levels, you will massively increase the likelihood of achieving them. Once you have aligned your levels, you will see how much easier the goal achieving part becomes.

So let's get started and explore what your very own core values are and how they affect every single decision you make.

Your Values

What are values?

VALUES CAN BE DEFINED AS broad preferences concerning appropriate courses of action or outcomes.

They help you distinguish right from wrong and they help you create a picture of "what should be."

Our values are established by a wide variety of factors, including our families and our cultures. Members of a specific culture often share similar values, and these values are often demonstrated by situations in which a person is honored or acknowledged.

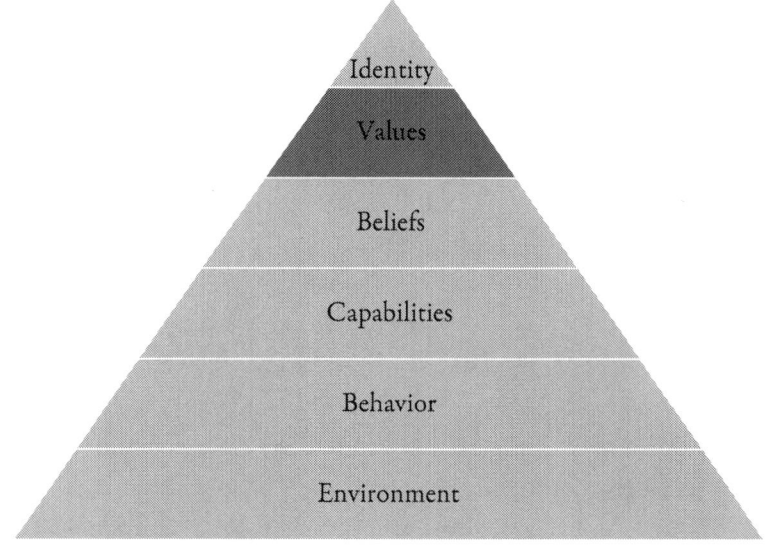

Definition of inner values (personal values)

> "The strongest principle of growth lies in human choice."
>
> — George Eliot

Personal values provide an internal reference point for what is good, beneficial, important, useful, beautiful, desirable, constructive, etc.

Every choice or decision we make, every action we take, and every behavior we demonstrate is based on our values. If we understand people's values, we will understand why people do what they do and how they prioritize what they do.

There are many ways to differentiate our value systems, for example personal core values and values of a company or a culture. The most useful one for our purpose is to divide our personal core values into two categories: Towards-to values and Away-from values.

You might say: This all sounds great, but how do I know what my own core values are?

Thanks for asking! Why don't we find that out in our next exercise?

Towards Values

Most of the people I talk with have only a vague idea of what is really important for them, and some of them have absolutely no idea what is important in their life. They are on auto-pilot. They do the tasks that they think they have to do, but all too often, they forget about the reasons behind what they do.

- WHY am I doing certain things?
- WHY do I prefer some tasks and avoid other ones?
- WHY am I so much quicker in performing xyz?

The answers are often found in your inner values. Therefore, one of the most valuable exercises you can do is to identify your inner values, your driving forces. I use a 5-step exercise to determine these values, and you can do the same right now to identify what you cognitively value most in life.

5-step value exercise

Step 1: What are the 3 most important personal values in your life? If you don't think you know the answer right now, then consider this question: What do you believe they should be to reflect who you are right now? Write them down now:

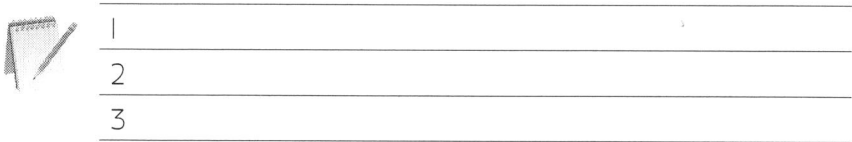

1
2
3

Step 2: Identify the values in the following list that best describe who you are right now. Pick as many as you feel would describe your values now:

Abundance	Acknowledgement	Alertness
Acceptance	Activeness	Altruism
Accessibility	Adaptability	Ambition
Accomplishment	Adventure	Amusement
Accountability	Affection	Anticipation
Accuracy	Aggressiveness	Appreciation
Achievement	Agility	Approachability

Articulacy	Closeness	Decisiveness
Assertiveness	Comfort	Deference
Assurance	Commitment	Delight
Attractiveness	Compassion	Democracy
Availability	Competence	Dependability
Awareness	Competition	Depth
Awe	Completion	Desire
Balance	Comprehension	Determination
Beauty	Concentration	Development
Being the best	Confidence	Devotion
Belonging	Conformity	Devoutness
Bliss	Congruency	Dignity
Boldness	Connection	Diligence
Bravery	Consciousness	Direction
Brilliance	Consistency	Directness
Calmness	Contentment	Discipline
Camaraderie	Continuity	Discovery
Capability	Contribution	Discretion
Care	Control	Diversity
Carefulness	Coolness	Dominance
Certainty	Cooperation	Dreaming
Challenge	Cordiality	Drive
Charity	Correctness	Duty
Charm	Courage	Dynamism
Chastity	Courtesy	Eagerness
Cheerfulness	Craftiness	Economy
Clarity	Creativity	Ecstasy
Cleanliness	Credibility	Education
Clear-mindedness	Curiosity	Effectiveness
Cleverness	Daring	Efficiency

Elegance	Flow	Humor
Empathy	Fluency	Hygiene
Encouragement	Focus	Imagination
Endurance	Fortitude	Impact
Energy	Frankness	Impartiality
Enjoyment	Freedom	Independence
Entertainment	Friendliness	Indulgence
Enthusiasm	Friendship	Influence on others
Excellence	Fun	Ingenuity
Excitement	Generosity	Inquisitiveness
Expectancy	Gentility	Insightfulness
Experience	Giving	Inspiration
Expertise	Grace	Integrity
Exploration	Gratitude	Intelligence
Expressiveness	Gregariousness	Intensity
Extroversion	Growth	Intimacy
Fairness	Guidance	Introversion
Faith	Happiness	Intuition
Fame	Harmony	Intuitiveness
Family	Health	Inventiveness
Fascination	Heart	Investing
Fashion	Helpfulness	Joy
Fearlessness	Heroism	Justice
Feeling of security	High spirit	Kindness
Fidelity	Holiness	Knowledge
Fierceness	Honesty	Leadership
Financial	Honor	Learning
Firmness	Hopefulness	Liberation
Fitness	Hospitality	Liberty
Flexibility	Humility	Life success

Liveliness	Perceptiveness	Reason
Logic	Perfection	Reasonableness
Longevity	Performance	Recognition
Love	Perseverance	Recreation
Loyalty	Persistence	Refinement
Lust for life	Personality	Reflection
Majesty	Persuasiveness	Relationship
Making a difference	Philanthropy	Relaxation
Market position	Piety	Reliability
Mastery	Playfulness	Religiousness
Maturity	Pleasantness	Reputation
Mindfulness	Pleasure	Resolution
Modesty	Poise	Resolve
Money	Polish	Resourcefulness
Motivation	Popularity	Respect
Mysteriousness	Potency	Responsibility
Neatness	Power	Rest
Nerve	Practicality	Restraint
Obedience	Pragmatism	Reverence
Objectivity	Precision	Richness
Open-mindedness	Preparedness	Sacredness
Openness	Presence	Sacrifice
Optimism	Privacy	Saintliness
Order	Proactivity	Satisfaction
Organization	Professionalism	Security
Originality	Prosperity	Self-control
Outlandishness	Prudence	Self-esteem
Outrageousness	Punctuality	Self-reliance
Passion	Purity	Self-respect
Peace	Realism	Selflessness

Sensitivity	Strength	Understanding
Sensuality	Structure	Uniqueness
Serenity	Success	Unity
Service	Support	Usefulness
Sexuality	Supremacy	Utility
Sharing	Surprise	Variety
Significance	Sympathy	Victory
Silence	Synergy	Vigor
Silliness	Teamwork	Virtue
Simplicity	Temperance	Vision
Sincerity	Thankfulness	Vitality
Skillfulness	Thoroughness	Vivacity
Sociability	Thoughtfulness	Warmth
Solidarity	Thrift	Watchfulness
Solitude	Tidiness	Wealth
Soundness	Timeliness	Willfulness
Speed	Tolerance	Willingness
Spirit	Traditionalism	Winning
Spirituality	Tranquility	Wisdom
Spontaneity	Transcendence	Wittiness
Stability	Trust	Wonder
Stealth	Trustworthiness	Youthfulness
Stillness	Truth	Zeal

Great! You can now transfer those you have marked here:

_____
_____
_____
_____
_____
_____
_____
_____
_____
_____
_____
_____
_____

Before you proceed with step 3 please check whether the three values of step 1 are included in your list. If not, just add them here so you can use them as well in step 3.

How many have you identified? 5? 10? 20? 30 or even more? Whatever number of values you came up with is great! The amount of values hugely varies from person to person. There is no right or wrong. These values are what you value in your life at this stage.

So again: Why should we care about values, and why was this an important exercise?

Every action we take, every decision we make and every behavior we demonstrate, is based on our values. Whenever we choose between alternatives, we invariably choose the one alternative which we value the most.

Step 3: Out of the complete list of all your own values, identify your TOP 8 values now.

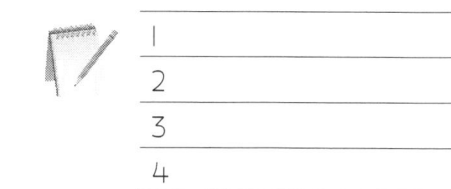

1.
2.
3.
4.
5.
6.
7.
8.

Just write down your most important, TOP 8 values in the fields above. Don't worry about putting them in order at this time; just make sure that you only list your 8 most important ones.

Step 4: Now think about the ranking of your TOP 8 values. Which ones are even more important than the others? Which should stay at the top of the list? Write the number 1-8 next to your values (1 being your #1 value, and 8 your 8th most important one).

Now transfer your ranked TOP 8 values to this table:

1.
2.
3.
4.
5.
6.
7.
8.

Step 5: Think of a recent goal you wanted or still want to achieve and ask yourself these questions:

- Which of my TOP 8 values does this goal support?

- Is this goal contradicting any of my TOP 8 values?

- If yes, can I scrap that goal or delegate it?

- And if not, what would I need to do to align this goal with my values?

The idea behind this exercise is to become aware of what your goals are, why you have them and how well they support your values. At this stage you only did the exercise for one goal. Later in this book, you will have plenty of opportunity to apply this strategy to all your important goals.

Congratulations! You just became crystal clear on your very own inner values! Knowing what you value most is a huge milestone on the journey of living a successful, meaningful and happy life.

Optional Step 6: Validating your value rankings with your subconscious mind

So far the value ranking steps have taken you through a very cognitive, mental approach to figuring out what you value the most. Almost all of my clients find these 5 steps to be extremely valuable and learn a lot through the process.

Additionally, I have achieved truly outstanding results with clients who are willing to examine the priorities of their values by asking specific questions directed to their subconscious mind. I will explain how this can be achieved, but I do not recommend that anyone try this on her/his own! If you are interested in these results, you should team up with an experienced coach who is familiar with such exercises and who is particularly trained in putting others into a trance state, so they can safely access the subconscious mind.

Sub-con	Con	Values
		A
		B
		C
		D
		E
		F
		G
		H

Values	A	B	C	D	E	F	G	H
Aggregate								
Sub-Conscious								

WHO ARE YOU AND WHY THIS IS IMPORTANT

This is a very powerful exercise I often offer to those of my clients who have great analytical skills and who are often more in their head than in touch with their emotions.

The setup is different from the steps before. We intentionally don't want to ask questions to our client, but we want to access their subconscious mind and get the intuitive, emotional answers, rather than the analytical ones we figured out in the steps before.

To achieve that, I often induce a trance-like alpha state with my client by using a different tone of voice and pace; I may also play meditative, calming background music.

Sub-con	Con	Values	
	1	Love	A
	2	Friends	B
	3	Health	C
	4	Family	D
	5	Financial Freedom	E
	6	Life Success	F
	7	Fun	G
	8	Learn and Grow	H

Values	A	B	C	D	E	F	G	H
Aggregate								
Sub-Conscious								

To gain a deeper understanding let's assume these are our TOP 8 values from the previous 5 steps.

Once an alpha-like trance state is reached, a coach then will describe 2 comparisons of the value pair, in our example here "Love" and "Friends".

For example: "Imagine, you would feel a very deep love to your spouse, your kids, your friends and this is a much more intense love than you ever experienced before. And those people also truly love you, unconditionally. And from now on, every day this intense feeling of love and being loved will get better and better. BUT at the same time: You would lose all your friends. They no longer want to be with you. And you also won't find any new, close friends in the future."

- This is the "pro A" scenario, because in this example, the value "Love" is in the 'A' column.

"Or, imagine you would develop a much deeper, honest and true connection to your close friends. And you would find some new, awesome friends who care for you no matter what. And every day, it gets better and better. You can have that BUT at the same time: You wouldn't feel true love for any other person, not your spouse, not for yourself, not even for your kids. And they also no longer love you…"

- This is the "pro B" scenario.

Then the coach asks a closed question: "Which scenario do you prefer: A or B?" Being in this alpha state the client doesn't have to think about the answer, but immediately feels what is right and whether he prefers A or B.

Of course, a good coach highly customizes the images and suggestions he describes to elicit what a client prefers if given the choice. You can easily see that a coach needs to be very sensitive and maintain a close rapport with the client during the entire session.

WHO ARE YOU AND WHY THIS IS IMPORTANT

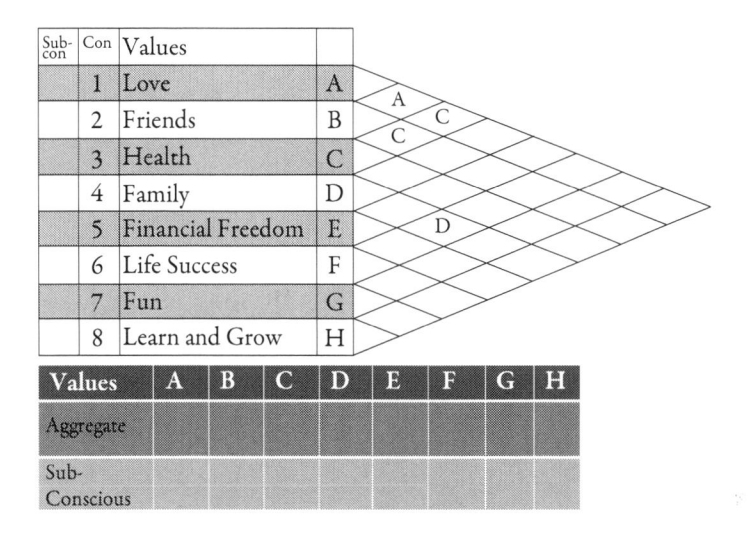

Sub-con	Con	Values	
	1	Love	A
	2	Friends	B
	3	Health	C
	4	Family	D
	5	Financial Freedom	E
	6	Life Success	F
	7	Fun	G
	8	Learn and Grow	H

Values	A	B	C	D	E	F	G	H
Aggregate								
Sub-Conscious								

Now, we would compare each value with every other one. In this example we first compared "Love" with "Friends". This imaginary client valued "Love" higher, so we put an "A" in the matrix.

When we compared "Love" with "Health," this client valued "Health" more, so we put down a "C," and so on. After comparing all these values and constantly keeping our client in this mild trance state, we would end up with a completely filled-in matrix, which could look like this:

Sub-con	Con	Values	
3	1	Love	A
4	2	Friends	B
1	3	Health	C
5	4	Family	D
8	5	Financial Freedom	E
6	6	Life Success	F
2	7	Fun	G
7	8	Learn and Grow	H

Values	A	B	C	D	E	F	G	H
Aggregate	4	4	7	3	0	3	6	1
Sub-Conscious	3	4	1	5	8	6	2	7

We then simply count how many times each letter appears, transfer the amount into the other table (row "Aggregate"), rank it accordingly from most important (1) to least important (8) and finally transfer these new results into the "Sub-Conscious"-column of the matrix.

We can see in this example and almost every time I did this exercise with my client, the new subconscious ranking differs quite substantially from the original, cognitive one.

Although this is an intense and very valuable 6th step of exploring your real inner values, it "only" questions the ranking of your consciously chosen core values.

Away-from values

Unlike with the towards-to values where you feel drawn to those core values which provide you with pleasant feelings, the away-from values are just the opposite: You try to avoid them; you try to move away from those on your list as you have previously associated some kind of pain or unpleasant feelings with them.

Remember that both categories are highly individual and whatever you come up with are your own values. This is especially true for your away-from values and other people could even have some of your away-from values on their towards-to list!

Exercise

Ask yourself the following questions and brainstorm a list of your away-from values:

↪ If you really want to achieve your ultimate purpose and your outcomes, what emotional states do you need to avoid indulging in?

↪ What have been the feelings in your past you would do almost anything to avoid having to feel?

And in a second step: Put those values in a hierarchy to answer the question:

⇨ Which away-from value do you need to avoid most in order to achieve your ultimate purpose?

If you have difficulties coming up with these away-from values, have a look at this non-comprehensive list of some common "Away-from" values.

Abandonment	Contempt	Failure
Anger	Deception	Frustration
Anxiety	Depression	Guilt
Bigotry	Disapproval	Helplessness
Blame	Dishonesty	Hopelessness
Cheating	Dismissed	Hostility
Conflict	Disrespectful	Humiliation
Complaining	Embarrassment	Hurt
Confusion	Egotistical	Ignorance

Indecisive	Nervous	Taken for granted
Inferiority	Out of Control	Tense
Insecure	Painful	Unimportant
Intimidating	Panicky	Unloved
Jealousy	Prejudiced	Victim-oriented
Loneliness	Rejection	Violent
Loss	Resentful	Weak
Negative	Shame	Worthless
Needy	Sorrowful	
Neglectful	Stressed	

Congratulations! You just gave yourself one of the most precious gifts you'll ever receive: Knowing what your current core values are is the first step to a more meaningful, fulfilled life!

Eventually you also noticed some values that aren't on your list yet but which you'd like to develop in the future to become your best self?

Knowing your values is wonderful. But in order to live up to your towards-to values and base your decisions on them: Wouldn't it be great to create some rules first that help you to be congruent with them?

That's exactly what we'll do next.

Exercise: Towards-to rules

Take your TOP towards-to values and ask yourself the following question:

What has to happen in order for you to feel [value 1; value 2; etc]? Find answers to every one of your TOP values.

Here are some tips and tricks

1. Make it very easy to constantly experience your core values. Start the rule by saying: "Anytime I ..."
2. Find a lot of different ways to experience your values and connect them with the word "or": "Anytime I do xyz, a) OR b) OR c) OR d) OR e)" ... this way, the rule becomes very easy to fulfill: as long as one of the 5 variables are true, you feel this value anytime!
3. Make sure you are in control: you alone determine your experience, not the outside world. So your rules shouldn't rely on other people to become reality.

EXAMPLE

Value: I move towards freedom.

Rules: I experience freedom anytime I
  a) am outside in nature OR
  b) look out the window OR
  c) take a deep breath and remind myself I can move anywhere OR
  d) think about my dreams and visualize how they manifest OR
  e) drive or fly to my favorite place on earth or just thinking about it.

We would like to avoid our away-from values. And in order to achieve this, we can make it very difficult to really experience them.

Exercise: Away from Rules

Take your TOP away-from values and ask yourself the following question:

What has to happen in order for you to feel [value 1; value 2; etc]? Find answers to every one of your TOP values.

Here are some tips and tricks

1. Make it very difficult to experience your Away-from values. You would have to do these rules consistently to experience the negative feeling.
2. Use the opposite technique now and say: "Only if I were to consistently..."
   a. "believe in the illusion that ... [I'm not good enough] AND
   b. "focus on the false belief that someone can ... [reject me] Then and only then you'd allow yourself to feel negative.
3. Come up with a solution for your Away Rules, i.e. "I avoid the consistent illusion of not being good enough"

> **EXAMPLE**
>
> Consistent inappropriate feeling of not being good enough
> Rules: Only if I were to consistently
>   a) believe in the illusion that I'm not good enough AND
>   b) I always fail to achieve my goals AND
>   c) never achieve anything important.
> Instead I realize that I have succeeded countless times again and again in many important aspects of my life.

Who do you need to become in your life?

> "We are not creatures of circumstance, we are creators of circumstance."
> — Benjamin Disraeli

You wouldn't have picked up this book if you didn't seriously want to develop yourself and strive to become your best self. Taking your elicited core values from the previous exercise, I would now like to invite you to think about who you ultimately want and need to become, so that you are super proud of who you are and that you live up to your full potential.

Take some time, make yourself comfortable, grab a cup of your favorite coffee and allow yourself to enjoy answering the following 6 questions:

1. What is your destiny?
    a. What kind of person do you ultimately want to become in your lifetime?

    _____
    _____
    _____
    _____
    _____

    b. What do you want your life to really be about?

    _____
    _____
    _____
    _____
    _____

2. What do your highest values need to be so that you will achieve your ultimate destiny?

    _____
    _____
    _____
    _____
    _____

Are these the same as in the 5 step exercise? Or are there some new values you feel you want to adopt?

3. Take your current TOP 8 core values and think about:
   a. What do you gain by having this value in this position on your list?

   b. What could it cost you to have this value in this position?

4. Which of your current core values do you need to eliminate in order to achieve your destiny?

5. What other values do you need to add in order to achieve your ultimate destiny?

6. And finally: What order do these new values need to be in, so that you will achieve your destiny?

Who are you at the end of your life?

> "I find that the great thing in this world is not so much where we stand as in what direction we are moving."
> — Oliver Wendell Holmes

In addition to the previous exercises, you might also want to picture yourself towards the end of your life. Imagine that you are reflecting back on all of your experiences.

- What are you most proud of?

_____
_____
_____
_____
_____
_____
_____

- What were the most meaningful moments?

_____
_____
_____
_____
_____
_____
_____

↪ Write down some of your thoughts from this perspective.

↪ What goals will you add to your list because of this experience?

↪ What have you accomplished in your professional life?

ME, MY BEST SELF AND I

- What was your family life like?

- Where have you traveled to?

- What were your hobbies?

Your Beliefs

> "If you think you can do a thing or think you can't do a thing, you're right."
>
> — Henry Ford

What are beliefs?

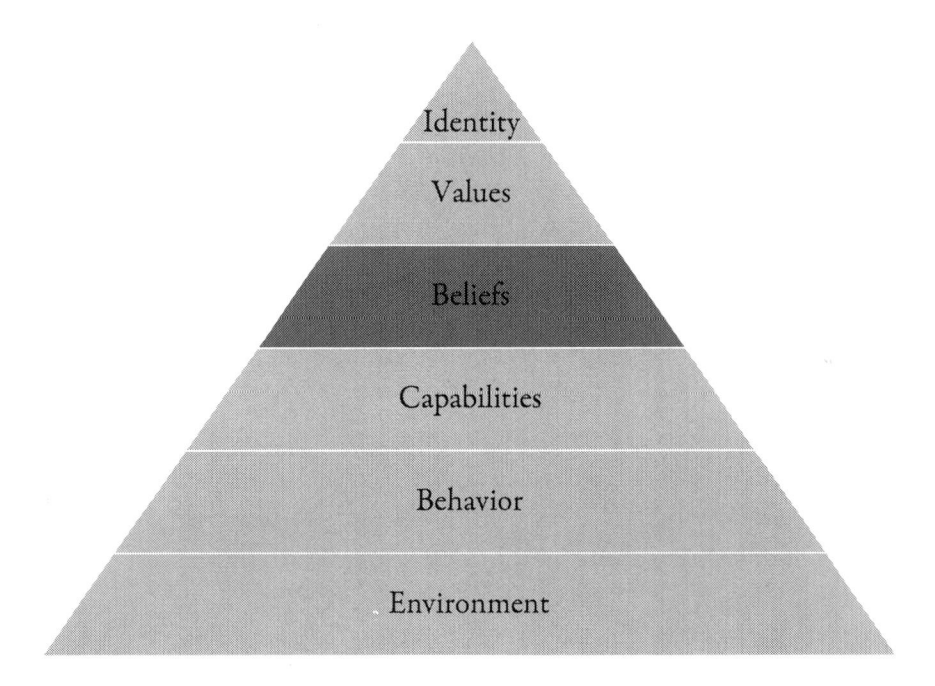

- Identity
- Values
- **Beliefs**
- Capabilities
- Behavior
- Environment

WHEN YOU ARE SERIOUS ABOUT transforming your dreams and desires into concrete, achievable goals and gaining a full understanding about these complex processes, it is not enough to just study the levels of behavior and skills. You have just seen what a powerful impact values have on you and whether you will achieve your goals. The next step is to understand how your beliefs will either serve as a stepladder to your goals, or as a roadblock. This chapter will help you clear out the roadblocks and create ladders where they might not have existed before.

We are not born with any beliefs; instead, we adopt them in the course of our lives. Therefore, beliefs can be changed, and as we will see, they can be changed quite easily.

Beliefs are an equally powerful and important aspect that will determine your success in achieving your goals and desires. Our beliefs determine who we are, how we act and what we think we are able to accomplish. Remember Henry Ford's bon mot: "If you believe you can or you believe you can't: You're always right."

Our beliefs come from different places, and sometimes we unquestionably adopt beliefs from other people. This is particularly true when we grow up and inherit the values and beliefs from our parents and later on from our teachers. Their model of the world becomes our model as well. Only at a later stage do we begin to question these beliefs and eventually "believe" in what we really find true for us.

As soon as a belief is created, we try to prove it through our action or inaction. This even happens with negative beliefs that we form, such as "I'm not good enough." The question now is, do our beliefs have to dictate our life or can we transform our negative beliefs?

When we accept that fact, or in other words: when we believe that our current beliefs and values are just a reflection of how we think, act and communicate today but they are not us, they are not our identity, then something very interesting happens: we open up to the possibility of changing certain beliefs that are limiting us and no longer serving our best interests whereas before that, we took these limiting beliefs for granted.

There is an example from the world of sports that shows exactly what can happen when we transform negative beliefs into positive ones. Up until 1954, everybody thought that running a mile in under four minutes was humanly impossible. However, on May 6th of that year, the world was in awe when Roger Bannister became the first person to run a mile in exactly 3 minutes and 59 seconds. The even more fascinating part though, is that many other runners were able to run the mile in less than 4 minutes in the very same year. What happened? How can we explain how all of a sudden many athletes were able to break through this invisible 4-minute barrier?

The best explanation is that they no longer maintained this belief that limited their potential. They no longer believed that it was impossible. In fact, they had proof that somebody did it. And so they quickly changed the old limiting belief into a positive one: "I can run the mile in less than 4 minutes, because Roger did it as well."

Never underestimate the power of your beliefs. The types of beliefs we have powerfully affect us.

We distinguish between 2 categories of beliefs:

1. Empowering beliefs
2. Limiting beliefs

The first category of our beliefs give us strength and allow us to achieve goals and reap positive benefits from our lives. In a recent research study, a group of people were given a survey asking them whether or not they believed they were healthy. Scientists found that there was a much stronger correlation between life expectancy and the person's beliefs than life expectancy and their actual health condition. The people that believed that they were healthy lived an average of seven years longer than the people who thought they were not healthy. In other words: take 2 identically healthy people at the same age and with the same life conditions: the one with the empowering belief of "I am healthy" lives 7 years longer than the one with the limiting belief of "I am not healthy".

In contrast to empowering beliefs, other beliefs limit our potential and take away our energy. These beliefs are roadblocks to our goals and may make us feel that we do not deserve success or the acceptance of others. We call these beliefs "Limiting Beliefs." They restrain us from reaching our goals and keep us confined to places that we do not want to be. You may have heard these types of beliefs before: "I am not good enough." Or "I don't do ____ very well." What goes in the blank when you hear these beliefs?

These limiting beliefs that hold us back have three types of messages.

- Despair: I cannot possibly achieve my goals.
- Powerlessness: My goal is possible, but I do not have the capacity to reach it.
- Unworthiness: I am not worthy of achieving my goals. I have done something or not done something that means that I do not deserve to achieve my goal.

Limiting beliefs often come from negative experiences in our lives. Consider the story of a girl who had always thought she was stupid, because her emotionally abusive father always told her that. Since she thought she was stupid, she didn't even try in high school, and eventually dropped out. After several years of aimlessness, she started to pursue her hobby of songwriting. She began to receive positive reinforcement from other musicians, which enabled her to replace her limiting belief that she was stupid with an empowering belief that she was an excellent songwriter. She now has an excellent career as a musician. At some stage in her life she transformed the limiting belief of not being good enough into a very empowering one.

The most important and sometimes also most difficult aspect of getting rid of negative beliefs is to identify them and understand them. This can be difficult because restraining beliefs become part of us, and it can be difficult to recognize the beliefs that limit our potential. As you think about some of your goals that you have failed to achieve in the past, try to expose restraining beliefs by asking targeted questions.

Why don't you believe that you can achieve your goals?

What abilities do you not have that would enable you to achieve your goal?

Why aren't you worthy of success with your goal?

If you honestly explore these questions, you can expose the restraining beliefs that are roadblocks to your goals. You will find that limiting beliefs come in clusters, so when you find one, keep prodding it to see if similar beliefs lie nearby. Your restraining beliefs will begin to lose their effect as soon as you identify them and begin to explore their origins.

Another important aspect of this process is to understand the purpose behind a limiting belief. Generally, our limiting beliefs fulfill purposes such as protecting us from something, or as an excuse for not doing something. For example, a common restraining belief for many people is "I am not good at public speaking." Thus they avoid seeking out professional opportunities or great networking possibilities that would help them achieve a goal. Instead, they could replace that belief with a positive message, i.e. "I do get nervous when I speak in public sometimes, which is great because I'm then fully aware and concentrated. The more I practice, the better and more confident I will become."

Both of these messages still protect the person from overly nerve-racking situations, but the second one encourages growth, while the first one completely limits growth.

It is important not only to identify our limiting beliefs, but also to acknowledge them for what they helped us to do or not to do in the past. From there we can move on and find a more suitable, more empowering belief which will serve us much better from now on.

Believe it or not: Exercises

Now what do you believe? Think about some of your own beliefs. What beliefs empower you? What beliefs restrain you? How and when did these beliefs form? How have they helped you so far? Which ones do you want to keep and strengthen and which ones do you want to replace?

Here are some easy exercises to start with:

Empowering beliefs:

> "Success is stumbling from failure to failure with no loss of enthusiasm."
> — Sir Winston Churchill

Finish these sentences:

1. I feel successful when:

    a.

    b.

    c.

2. I am truly fulfilled when:

    a.

    b.

    c.

3. I feel needed when:

   a.

   b.

   c.

These answers might give you hints of some of your empowering beliefs. Think about why you have already achieved so many outstanding goals in your life? What was it that let you follow through, sometimes against all odds? What did you believe to achieve them?

Identify your current TOP 5 empowering beliefs:

1
2
3
4
5

Wow. Congratulations! You have now identified some of your most powerful beliefs that are the driving forces for your behavior. They let you achieve the goals you really want.

As a next step you might want to rehearse them over and over again so that these 5 empowering beliefs become your personal truth. You truly believe in them and you want to let all your decisions and behavior be influenced by these empowering beliefs.

A great way to not only rehearse those rules but to actually instill those beliefs deep into your body, is to use the technique of incantations where you fully engage your whole body in not only saying but acting this belief as if it is the most important true thing in your life. You can sing and shout, dance, make power movements and do whatever comes to your mind to support this empowering belief. Do this bodily exercise over and over again as if you wanted to convince your worst critic that you actually mean what you believe. Once you have repeated it a dozen times a day for several days, it will start to become a habit. And as soon as it becomes a habit, it will positively and automatically influence the actions you will take.

Example: "I have an abundance of enthusiasm and passion in my life now."

This is one of my own empowering beliefs that I repeat over and over again in my morning incantation ritual.

In the next step, let's explore some of your limiting beliefs and explore whether you might want to change them.

Limiting beliefs:

Identify your TOP 5 limiting beliefs

1 _____
2 _____
3 _____
4 _____
5 _____

Now it is time to express a little warning about the next exercise. Make sure you have at least an hour of uninterrupted time and a calm place you can concentrate easily.

The following exercises can be very stressful, especially when you fully engage with them and exercise them thoroughly, which of course I highly encourage you to do. This is on purpose and very valuable for the later progression. I deliberately invite you to engage yourself fully into these questions and feel the pain these limiting beliefs are causing you. The more you do, the more leverage you will later have to never again feel those emotions.

For each limiting belief, ask yourself:

    a. What have they cost me?
    b. What are the most negative consequences for me if I don't change them?
    c. What have I missed out on?
    d. Who did I hurt?
    e. Who is not in my life because of it?
    f. What will it ultimately destroy?

Answer each of this question for each of your limiting beliefs for your past, for right now and for the future.

So as an example: If one of our limiting beliefs is "I'm not good enough!", then we ask: What has this limiting belief cost me in the past? What does it cost me right now (i.e. what am I not doing, having, being etc. because of this belief)? And what will it cost me in the future?

Allow yourself to feel the pain and accept every strong emotion that eventually pops up once you uncover specific answers.

Exercise

Limiting belief I:	
What has it cost me?	Past: Now: Future:
What are the most negative consequences for me if I don't change it?	Past: Now: Future:
What have I missed out?	Past: Now: Future:
Who did I hurt?	Past: Now: Future:
Who is not in my life because of it?	Past: Now: Future:
What will it ultimately destroy?	Past: Now: Future:

Limiting belief II:	
What has it cost me?	Past:
	Now:
	Future:
What are the most negative consequences for me if I don't change it?	Past:
	Now:
	Future:
What have I missed out?	Past:
	Now:
	Future:
Who did I hurt?	Past:
	Now:
	Future:
Who is not in my life because of it?	Past:
	Now:
	Future:
What will it ultimately destroy?	Past:
	Now:
	Future:

Limiting belief III:	
What has it cost me?	Past: Now: Future:
What are the most negative consequences for me if I don't change it?	Past: Now: Future:
What have I missed out?	Past: Now: Future:
Who did I hurt?	Past: Now: Future:
Who is not in my life because of it?	Past: Now: Future:
What will it ultimately destroy?	Past: Now: Future:

Now that you have finished this exercise: How do you feel? Chances are that you feel some form of pain or anger in your body. This is a good thing!

The more pain you associated with your limiting beliefs the more you are now willing to change these beliefs so you never again experience this kind of pain.

So let's move on and explore three strategies to reframe these limiting beliefs and ultimately set them straight as what they are: limiting you in becoming your best self!

Changing limiting beliefs: Reframing them into empowering beliefs

> "I've missed more than 9000 shots in my career. I've lost almost 300 games. Twenty-six times, I've been trusted to take the game-winning shot and missed. I've failed over and over and over again in my life. And that is why I succeed."
>
> — Michael Jordan

There are several ways of reframing or changing a limiting and often negative belief into an empowering, positive belief. These are my favorite 3 methods.

1. Intellectually questioning the truth of that belief
2. Reframing it by using powerful incantations
3. Changing the sub-modalities of a limiting belief

Intellectually questioning the truth of that belief

We can intellectually explore the WHYs of our limiting belief until we understand that most of our limiting beliefs are ridiculous. This is the most common and easiest way to change a limiting belief. When you identify a limiting belief, you can ask yourself these simple questions:

Is this really so? Is it really true? And Is this always the case?

First, you will probably tell yourself "Of course that is true!" and you might even name three examples. But if you really think about it, you will quickly realize that it is not entirely true.

It is very common that people I work with have the limiting belief that they are not good enough. And they can always tell me two, three or sometimes more "stories" supporting this belief. But is this really true? And is this always the case? Can there be anybody in the world who is simply not good enough for anything? No! It is just a story we keep telling ourselves. And worse: it is simply a lie. There are hundreds if not thousands of things where we are absolutely good enough to perform them.

When you have this belief that you are not worthy, for example, simply reframe your belief. Ask yourself: Am I really not good enough to live in this world (I have never done anything right) or was I just not capable or not willing to perform a certain task or challenge at a specific time in a specific environment?

Even at this stage, people often realize that their original story of not being good enough is of course not true. But to demonstrate how wrong this common limiting belief is, push yourself further by naming 10 specific situations where you felt you were not good enough or when you felt rejected. Chances are you will hardly come up with five situations. And the next question would be to name 10 specific situations that occurred yesterday, where you succeeded with the task at hand (getting up, preparing breakfast, cleaning the kitchen, getting to work, etc.).

The few times that people with this limiting belief really felt rejected or not good enough have primed them to believe that they as a person were not good enough. The truth is of course, that only in a few situations have they felt incapable of performing a desired outcome.

So most people will realize after a few minutes of talking about their limiting beliefs, that they are not true and that there are millions of other examples that prove these limiting beliefs are wrong.

Reframing it by using powerful incantations

In the first step, we write down the old limiting belief for the very last time. We then take a different pen and scratch it out several times until we can barely read it.

We then reframe it into a more positive, empowering belief. In our example, instead of "I'm not good enough" we could write: "I am really good in all things that matter to me!"

So we didn't just reverse the old belief into its opposite, because our conscious mind might have strong objections against the complete opposite. Instead, we reframed it in a way that our mind can easily accept this new belief as our new truth.

Once we have created such a compelling, empowering belief, we then can use the power of incantations (as described in detail in the previous chapter) to instill this new belief deep inside our whole body and to make it become an automatic habit. After a few weeks of practicing these incantations, you will wonder how you could ever have believed your old "truth".

Changing the sub-modalities of a limiting belief

A sub-modality is the way we process information we get from our senses. Therefore, everybody's experience of a particular thing is different, depending on how we process and represent sensory information. Thus your experience is determined not so much by what you perceive from your senses, but by how you process, store, interpret and represent this information, or your sub-modalities.

We have five basic senses which we also can call modalities: visual, auditory, kinesthetic, olfactory and gustatory. For each of these modalities, we can have finer and more detailed distinctions.

For example, we could describe a picture as being black and white or colorful. It could also be bright or dim. Sounds could be loud or soft, or coming from a particular direction. Feelings could be in different parts of the body or have different temperatures. Smells could be pleasant or offensive, strong or light. Taste could be sweet or bitter or strong or mild. These finer distinctions are called sub-modalities and define the qualities of our internal representations.

While some sub-modalities might make you feel excited or happy, when you run other sub-modalities, you might feel angry or hurt.

What does this mean to you as far as limiting and empowering beliefs? By changing the sub-modalities you use to represent an experience, you can adjust your feelings about a particular experience. So when you identify a limiting belief, you can actually change the sub-modalities you use to represent it with.

As an example, let's imagine someone whose primary sense is visual. If this person has a limiting belief of not being good enough, he might picture himself in such a situation. He sees a large, colorful image of himself in front of his eyes, doing something "not good enough". So his visual sub-modalities are very vivid which doesn't help for this particular situation, since the clearer and brighter he sees this picture the more pain he feels while thinking about this limiting belief.

If he wants to change his reaction to this limiting belief, he could simply change these visual sub-modalities. For example, he could make this picture of him not being good enough black and white, shrinking the size of this picture, and maybe letting it look blurred as well, or even adding a comical soft-focus effect.

This way, the next time he gets the feeling of "not being good enough" he will remember the new image with the altered sub-modalities: less scary, maybe even funny.

Now that you have identified your current empowering beliefs as well as your limiting beliefs and how you might want to change them, let's move on and explore whether you want to instill some additional empowering beliefs. We have seen that once we are aware of beliefs, we can actively choose what we believe in. And the more often and more intense we believe in something, the sooner it becomes a habit and very often a self-fulfilling prophecy.

Think about some additional empowering beliefs you'd like to add to your portfolio

1. _____
2. _____
3. _____
4. _____
5. _____

Ideally, all of our beliefs are in line with our values and our identity. If not, they will often prevent us from becoming our best self because of these conflicting values and beliefs. Both positive and negative beliefs tend to become true because our subconscious mind is programmed to help our beliefs become self-fulfilling prophecies.

As you have seen, a good starting point for anyone who wants to achieve their goals and live up to their full potential is to become aware of your beliefs: both limiting and empowering. And once you encounter stories that you are telling yourself and others, ask yourself these powerful questions:

1. Is this really so?
2. What else can that mean?

By now you have seen that there are basically just two factors that make people do what they do… and do not do: Their values and their beliefs.

In fact these two are so powerful, they control all of our thoughts, emotions, decisions and actions! They are the blueprint of our lives.

Your Desires

Now we get to one last, yet very important aspect that will factor into whether or not you will achieve your outcomes: your desires. You cannot possibly hope to achieve a goal if you don't really desire to. Consider Napoleon Hill's words:

> "The starting point of all achievement is desire. Keep this constantly in mind. Weak desires bring weak results, just as a small amount of fire makes a small amount of heat."
> — Napoleon Hill

How much desire do you have to achieve your goal?

The key for a fulfilled, successful life is to align your everyday behavior, actions and decisions you make with who you are, your identity, your values, your beliefs and your desires. As you become more congruent and increase the alignment between these four levels, you will be able to achieve your goals more easily. Desire plays such an important role in determining our goals, because we are constantly confronted in life with choices between pursuing one goal or another. Many people come to a point in their professional lives where they must choose between their goals of immediate financial wellbeing and pursuing an alternative career. Making one decision almost always has certain opportunity-costs involved:

those missed opportunities that you could also have chosen. Though we encounter many difficult decisions, it is important to pursue goals that help us get the most out of life, so individual values and desires should play an important role in determining which goals to pursue.

Use the exercises in this book to help you determine if all of the factors that go into achieving goals are aligned in your life: values, beliefs, desires. You will have little chance of success if each of these three things aren't working together. You may value and desire a certain goal, but if your beliefs about what you can do don't support that, then you will likely not succeed.

I'd like to encourage you to question your current status quo and particularly your values and beliefs. More often than not, people are positively surprised the moment they realize that certain beliefs are no longer necessary. Or that "new" values have become important in their lives and have a massive influence on their decisions.

It has happened over and over again, that participants of my Breakthrough-Workshops seemed to know what they wanted to achieve. They formulated a goal. They even applied the SMART goals formula. But unless they were 100% clear on their own core values and what they truly desire, those goals were of little value.

Why? Because more often than not they realized that some of their goals don't support their most important values. And even worse: sometimes they had to admit, that some of their goals even contradicted their values. For those cases, it is obvious that they couldn't achieve their goal as easily, and if they did, it was only at the high cost of not living congruently and aligned with their values.

> **EXAMPLE**
>
> Consider Mike's story: Mike was a Vice President with a Frankfurt-based Financial Institution. He was very ambitious, well-educated and after 10 years in the industry he knew what needed to be done to climb the corporate ladder. One of his goals was to become a Managing Director in his firm and he worked very hard to achieve this outcome.
>
> At the same time he asked himself one question over and over again: Is that it? Being promoted every few years and staying in this industry?
>
> He had another desire: To become an entrepreneur and start his own consultancy firm where he could use all his experience and passion to make a real difference in his clients' lives.
>
> The obvious challenge for him was to make a decision whether to fully concentrate and focus on his corporate, relatively safe job or to make the move towards an unknown, exciting but also risky new endeavor.
>
> His desire for a new challenge, for trying it himself, for defying the odds was in direct conflict with one of his top values: Security. Being able to provide for his family, paying the bills, maintaining his ambitious lifestyle.
>
> Such conflicts of certain core values with one's own desires and beliefs often generates a lot of discomfort, stress and often plenty of fear.
>
> One way out of this dilemma for Mike was to become aware of his own values and beliefs as well as his desires. And to align them in a way where he could live congruently without violating any major value, belief or desire.

Imagine, WHAT IF: Visualizing who you want to be (come)

> "If you can dream it, you can do it."
> — Walt Disney

Dreams really do come true. People who visualize that they will achieve their goals are more likely to achieve success. So take a second to think about your goals and the exercises you have done in this book so far. Now imagine what it might feel like to accomplish those goals. What would it feel like to achieve your desires? What would it feel like to exactly know what your values are and live in alignment with them? What would it feel like to fulfill your desires?

Highly successful businessman Lee Iacocca once said, "The greatest discovery of my generation is that human beings can alter their lives by altering their attitudes of mind." Do you want to alter your life? Then how will you alter your attitude? To help yourself visualize the goal, find an image or a tangible object that you can look at every day to help remind you of the goal. For example, someone who is hoping to get back into running shape might visualize a medal that they got a long time ago for a running achievement. A person who is trying to lose weight might visualize their goal with an item of clothing they would like to fit into. The benefit of this technique is that it helps us visualize our goal.

Top Athletes are often highly skilled in visualizing precisely not only what and why they want to achieve a certain success. Many are particularly good in visualizing how they are going to achieve it.

Take one of the most successful luger of all time, three time Olympic and World Champion Georg Hackl. Immediately before any race, he visualized every single turn of the bobsled run. And not only that, he experienced the whole race in his mind even before he started, by closing his eyes and making the same movements with his head as he'd later do in the sled. And that's all in real-time. You can say: he won (or lost) a race even before it started.

Or think about any of the Top 100 golfers in the world; they all have an individual pre-shot routine, which is 5-10 times longer than the actual shot. They visualize in great detail how the ball will fly (or roll on the putting green), where it will land and where the ball will come to a stop.

2
WHAT do you really, really want to achieve in your life?

Something to think about

WHAT WOULD HAPPEN IF I call you tomorrow morning at 3am and ask you about your goals you are most passionate about? Would you need to think about it? Or shout them out with a huge smile on your face?

Most people can tell you exactly what they don't want or what they want less in their lives. And that is a good starting point. But to become your best self it is vital to also know exactly what you really, really want from and in your life. In fact the starting place for anybody who wants to achieve ambitious goals is to figure out what those goals are. It is literally impossible to achieve goals if you do not know what your goals are in the first place. Just think of you as being the captain of a nice sailing ship in the middle of a beautiful, calm ocean. You can go anywhere you want. But if you don't know where you want to go, and you change course every few days: you will never reach any destination.

So let's get started. Take a few minutes and answer the following questions:

Exercise: Status Quo

What are your goals? Think of previous goals you set for yourself. Small ones, big ones, any goals you thought you would like to achieve at one point.

WHAT DO YOU REALLY, REALLY WANT TO ACHIEVE IN YOUR LIFE?

What makes you happy?

Where do you want be ten years down the road? How should your life look? Who is with you? What do you do and not do any longer?

How do you want to impact the world and the people around you?

How do you want others to remember you?

Now for the really tough question: Are your daily actions leading you towards all of these things that you aspire towards?

Fantastic! Congratulations on answering these questions honestly, as they will set you in the right state to get the maximum out of the next chapters.

Needs vs Wants

DID YOU NOTICE THE TITLE of this chapter: "What do you really, really want to achieve?" I have emphasized the "really" as it makes a lot of sense to discover not only what you think would be great to have or to become, but what you absolutely MUST have or become. Really!

I also could have underlined the word "want". Why?

We all have certain human needs which we constantly strive to fulfill. I'll explain the six most basic human needs we all have in common in a moment. At this stage let me state one of my own core beliefs very clearly: Nobody needs to change, nobody needs to achieve anything and nobody needs to read this book or any other self-empowering book.

Seriously, you don't need to do that. Since you are not broken, you don't need to be fixed.

Here is what you and I and everybody else really needs. We all need a certain degree of

- Certainty & Security
- Uncertainty & Variety
- Love & Connection
- Significance
- Growth
- Contribution

Anthony Robbins made this human need psychology popular. We all need to feel safe and comfortable; experience exciting new things; feel loved by and connected to others; feel special and worthy of attention; grow, develop and learn and contribute beyond ourselves.

This is true for all of us. The only difference is in which order these needs apply to the people. Many rank "Certainty & Security" and "Love & Connection" as their top needs. Others value "Growth" and "Significance" higher. Any combination is possible, there is no right or wrong. You can learn a lot about yourself and others by simply assessing your own order of these needs or for people you are interacting with.

While it is very useful to know your own needs and in which order you "need" them to be fulfilled, there is another layer of information which in my experience is even more important. This is where the chapter title comes into play. What do you actually want?

WHAT DO YOU REALLY, REALLY WANT TO ACHIEVE IN YOUR LIFE?

It may sound like a profane question but think of it again: Do you really know, what exactly you want from your life?

Very different to the human need psychology, the things people value most highly differ within from what I call the "Human Want Psychology". So instead, there are three questions with which we can elicit what we really want:

1. For each of your life areas, what do you think would you like to do or possess that it adds to your well-being and help you become your best self?
2. Why exactly do you believe this?
3. For each want you identify, how exactly would it make you feel better?

Now that we established a basic idea of what we need and what we want, let's move on and transform those ideas into concrete, measurable goals.

3
The science of effective goal setting

> "If a man knows not what harbor he seeks, any wind is the right wind."
> — Seneca

What are goals anyway?

> "Goals are dreams with deadlines."
> — Diana Scharf Hunt

A GOAL OR OBJECTIVE IS a desired result a person envisions, plans and commits to achieve. It might be personal or organizational in nature, and it describes a desired endpoint.

We should not confuse goals with dreams and desires. Whereas dreams and desires can be extremely powerful, often being highly emotional and a great driving force, they rarely materialize by dreaming or desiring them alone. But if we transform our dreams into very concrete goals while keeping the associated great feelings and our enthusiasm: magic can and does happen.

Unfortunately, our dreams don't always become reality. Conscious and intentional planning for each step of a goal gives us a much better chance of success and provides us with a way to actually measure our success. Effective personal goals can and should be broken down into manageable steps along the journey. We will talk about this in detail later.

Step-by-step planning and execution is a highly efficient way for our goals to come to fruition. Though this step-by-step method of planning and achieving goals is not complicated in the slightest, I rarely meet a person who has committed to follow through on all the important outcomes.

As an example, imagine that you are planning a move. You need to plan your approach by researching places you would like to move, looking for job possibilities, and researching housing options. Once your housing and employment are in place, you will need to pack and hire movers. After completing these steps, you will have successfully relocated. If you want to fulfill your goals, you must follow a similar process.

But what does this process look like as far as setting goals? Just like with planning the move, you have to follow a series of small steps.

Now why should we care about goal setting in the first place?

I'm pretty sure you know the power and value of thoughtful goals already. Let me share just one study with you, which really says it all.

It is said that a study at Harvard reveals exactly why it is so critical that you set precise goals and write them down. In 1979, Harvard MBA students were surveyed about their goal setting habits. 84% did not have any specific goals at all, 13% had goals but had not written them down, and only 3% had clear goals in writing and a plan for how to accomplish them. That in itself is quite interesting. Only 3% of Harvard MBAs had precise goals!

Now here is the most interesting part: Ten years later, researchers found that the ones who had written down their goals were earning on average, ten times as much as the other 97 percent put together.

Knowing these statistics, who doesn't want to belong to the 3%, eh?

Dreams and Desires Exercise

> "Dream no small dreams for they have no power to move the hearts of men."
> — Johann Wolfgang von Goethe

Write down a list of your dreams and desires which you would like to accomplish before you die. Enjoy this process, and allow yourself to feel inspired and dream big. And later on you can decide to transform them into actionable goals:

Lifecycle of a goal

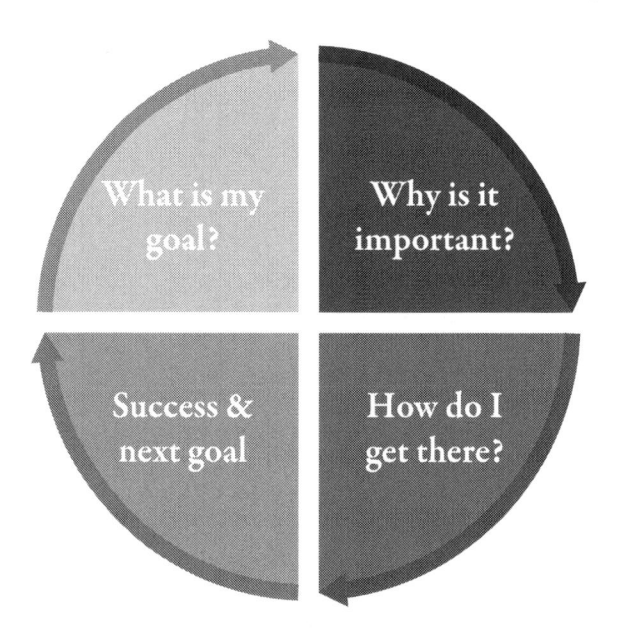

(Diagram: A circular cycle with four quadrants — "What is my goal?", "Why is it important?", "How do I get there?", "Success & next goal".)

The number one reason why people don't follow through on their New Year's Resolutions, struggle with their ambitious outcomes or do not achieve their goals at all is this:

After they think they know what they want, they immediately start acting on it. And they skip 2 very important questions. The first is the reason WHY they want to achieve it. And the second is to develop a game plan and commit to it or in other words: HOW they will achieve their goal.

The reason why I'm writing about "people" in general is that you obviously do not belong to this group, right? But I'm sure you know somebody in your inner circle. Since you followed the exercises in chapter 1 I'm sure you are very certain about your reason why by now.

Then let's spend some time together and explore the science of effective goal setting.

The importance of clear goals

IMAGINE THAT YOU DIDN'T HAVE any goals in your life. What would you do right now (probably stop reading this book)? What would your day look like? What would this year look like? What would your whole life look like? And then how would you feel if you knew you make 35,000 decisions every single day?

You simply can't know where you're going without having clear goals.

> **EXAMPLE**
>
> Do you remember the wonderful adventures of Alice in Wonderland? Alice once asked Cheshire Cat: "'Would you tell me, please, which way I ought to go from here?"
> "That depends a good deal on where you want to get to."
> "I don't much care where."
> "Then it doesn't matter which way you go."
> "So long as I get SOMEWHERE."
> "Oh, you're sure to do that, if you only walk long enough."
> Without goals you will be just like Alice, heading towards somewhere. But who knows where that somewhere will end up being. Setting goals is the first thing you must do if you want to have some say in where that "somewhere" is. Goals establish the direction and the blueprints for our lives.

But since you are way more determined than Alice, you of course know where to go, right? Let's see where you are at this stage. Think about your TOP 5 goals of last year.

Alice Exercise:

- What have been your most important goals last year?

  1 _____
  2 _____
  3 _____
  4 _____
  5 _____

- How many and which of them have you achieved?

  _____
  _____
  _____
  _____

- How many and which of them have you NOT achieved?

  _____
  _____
  _____
  _____

- Why haven't you achieved some of them?

  _____
  _____
  _____
  _____

Top 10 reasons WHY you should set crystal clear goals

Setting goals is critical for many reasons, but above all setting goals helps you determine what decisions, behaviors and which actions you should take to enjoy the journey towards living your purpose.

1	Setting goals enables you to determine who you are in the world. Without goals, you can hope to be who you want to be, but you are not sitting in the driver seat to determine those actions that must happen so that you shape your own destiny.
2	Setting goals establishes a purpose for your life. Goals are ideally a reflection of your inner values, beliefs and desires which will give you direction.
3	Setting goals gives you confidence. When you reach a goal, you give yourself a confidence boost and improve your chance of success in reaching future goals.
4	Setting goals gives you a positive outlook. Goals help you establish momentum to move in a positive direction.
5	Setting goals allows you to see that what you thought was impossible before now is possible. Rather than thinking of your goals as things you might "someday, maybe" accomplish, you can use "chunking" to break your goals into manageable chunks to accomplish within a certain time frame.
6	Setting goals will expand your comfort zone. When we set challenging goals, we inherently stretch ourselves to grow and do things we might not normally have done. Growth only takes place in our stretch zone, just outside of our comfort zone.
7	Your Goals Define You. You know the saying: "Tell me who you hang out with and I will tell you if you will be able to achieve your goals and dreams." The same is true for this: "Show me your goals, and I will tell you whether you will achieve them."

8	Setting goals will help you believe in your decisions. It can be easy to succumb to peer pressure and pursue things that others want you to pursue. However, your purpose and your goals will keep you grounded and help you make decisions that will be aligned with your values, beliefs and desires.
9	Setting goals will help you feel satisfied. People who set goals reach higher levels of satisfaction in their lives, because they accomplish more, they can clearly relate their efforts to their accomplishments, and they continue to make new goals.
10	Setting goals helps you become more reliant on yourself. When you take control of your life, you will not be nearly so dependent on others.

We can easily see all the benefits of goal setting. We will soon get to the nitty-gritty details of how to set proper goals. But even if you constantly define very precise goals, it's a whole different story to actually achieve them.

There are thousands of good reasons, excuses or simply stories why someone could not or would not achieve a specific goal. In the next chapter we will explore some of the most common reasons why goals aren't achieved, so that we can learn how to conquer these excuses. The following list is by no means exhaustive, rather it should give you a quick overview of how you can avoid stepping into a goal-avoidance trap.

Top 10 reasons WHY goals are often not achieved

1	When your goal is not aligned with your values, beliefs and desires. We already discussed the importance of values and desires in achieving goals. When your goals are not aligned with them, it becomes almost impossible to achieve them.
2	When you do not make consistent progress towards goals. When you stop making progress towards your goal, you not only lose momentum but run the risk of losing your goal altogether. This is why you need to devote at least a little bit of time every day to moving your goal forward.
3	When you are not fully committed. Sometimes we set goals that we don't really care about achieving. Maybe we set the goal because we thought we should or because somebody else wanted us to. These goals don't usually stand much of a chance.
4	When your goals do not inspire you. If your goal doesn't make you feel excited, then the odds are not likely that you will achieve it. Aim for goals that really make you excited.
5	When you lose your focus. It can be easy to lose focus on our goals as we try to move through our daily life. This is why you have to constantly remind yourself of your goals and plant visual and tangible reminders in your life.
6	When you do not write down your goals. Remember that Harvard study where the 3% of participants who wrote down their goals were earning ten times as much as those who did not? Enough said.
7	When you don't focus your goals in a positive way. Create goals that are focused on achieving a positive outcome. If you are unhappy in your current job, you are much more likely to achieve your goal if you focus on landing your dream job than if you focus on being able to quit your old job.
8	When we follow an impulse rather than our strategic goals. A prime example of following an impulse instead of our goal is if we make a goal to lose weight, but then cannot resist temptations to overeat. We opt for immediate gratification rather than long-term satisfaction.

9	Goals are not formulated according to SMART principles. SMART goals are those that are specific, measurable, attractive, realistic and timely. SMART goals tend to give you a laser focus and keep you on track.
10	Goals do not follow the 4 MOVE rules. You should not have too many goals; they should be your own; they should reflect your values; and they should be exclusive.

How can you easily avoid all 10 of those traps and basically every important one I can think of? Simply understand and learn to always make a "SMART MOVE" whenever you define and work on your goals. In the next chapter we will explore how a SMART MOVE looks like.

Before we move on to the next chapter, try to remember some of your "strategies" you have used to NOT achieve some of your goals:

What else gets in the way of achieving your goals? List your own reasons why you procrastinate, defer, ignore or sabotage your goals.

How to Set Effective Goals

BECAUSE YOU ARE READING THIS book now, I will assume a few character traits that we share in common:

We want to grow and achieve our outcomes. We all want to have a significant impact on the world and live to the fullest. When we set goals, we are vowing to work towards personal growth and development. We dedicate ourselves to putting forth the effort for the duration of a project and not allowing ourselves to make excuses for not following through with our plan.

To achieve our goals, it is important to recognize and deal with the things that hold us back, such as limiting beliefs or conflicting values that will impede our quest. It is also important to break goals down into small steps so that you can have the experience of achieving a short-term goal. Achieving a clearly articulated goal leads to strong feelings of accomplishment and can help you find purpose in your daily grind.

SMART Goals

If you are serious about setting ambitious and yet achievable goals, you should start with a very simple exercise: write down your goals. All of them! Remember the Harvard Study? Only 3% of the Harvard MBA students wrote their goals down and 10 years later, they earned 10 times as much as the other 97% combined.

Now that you have seen how powerful written goals are:

What are the criteria for efficiently formulated goals?

If you really want to achieve your goals, they should be:

- Specific
- Measurable
- Attractive
- Realistic
- Timely

Now how many times have you heard/read that? Well, here comes the kicker: How regularly do you apply this basic SMART formula to your goals? How about this: make today the day where you once and for all start using this formula every time you set new goals for yourself.

Let's do a quick recap of the 5 SMART rules:

Specific

Start your goal setting by formulating your goals in a specific way, since specific goals have a much greater chance of success than general goals. These 5 questions will help you be more specific:

*Why: What are your reasons and purpose for wanting to achieve this goal? How will it benefit you?

*What: What exactly do you hope to accomplish?

*Who: Who else will be involved in achieving this goal?

*When: When will you achieve the goal in its entirety? When will you achieve each individual step?

*Which: Which constraints and requirements will affect how you pursue your goal?

Let's look at an example to help us illustrate the difference between a general goal and a specific goal. A general goal would be, "I want to lose weight." But a specific goal would say, "I want to lose 5 kg within the next 3 months."

Being specific is very important, because when you are vague, you will not know whether you have made progress. If your goal is "I want to earn more money," my reply would be "I'll give you this dollar and now let's get out of here." Is that what you wanted? No? Then how will you craft a SMARTer goal?

Measurable

You can only manage what you can measure. Establish concrete parameters for measuring progress toward the attainment of each of your goals. When you measure your progress, you stay on track, reach your target dates, and experience these motivating emotions when you know you are on a great path to achieve your goals.

To determine if your goal is measurable, ask these questions:

How much? How many?

How will I know when it is accomplished?

> EXAMPLE (for losing weight): I need to know my current weight as a starting point, and commit myself to weighing in every Monday, so I can measure my progress.

A long time ago, the word "goal" implied that there was a measurable outcome. This does work well when something quantifiable can be tied to the goal. However, there are plenty of worthy goals that may not have quantifiable aspects, such as becoming part of a community in a new place that you have moved. If you were to focus on the measurable aspects of this goal, you may lose sight of what really matters in establishing a community. Depending on the nature of your goal, make an appropriate decision as to whether or not a measurable outcome will be helpful.

Attractive

Goals need to be attractive. Now in contrast to the specific and measurable aspects of a goal, which clearly are objective and can be reviewed by others, whether or not a goal is attractive to you is purely subjective. Though we all have subjective perceptions of what is attractive, you will be much more committed to achieving a goal when you deem it attractive.

> **EXAMPLE**
>
> Losing weight might be attractive for a lot of people, but others might want nothing more than to gain weight. For those people, the initial goal is not at all attractive.

To determine if your goal is attractive to you, ask these questions:

- How would you feel if you had already achieved this goal?
- What if you didn't achieve it? How bad would you feel? What would be missing?
- Why do you feel you MUST achieve this goal?

Realistic

To be realistic, a goal must represent an objective towards which you are both willing and able to work. Being realistic doesn't mean that you should aim for lower goals just to be on the safe side. It's just the opposite. A goal can very well be both ambitious and realistic. You are the only one who can decide just how high your goal should be. Whether your goal is realistic or not is a highly subjective point of view.

An ambitious goal is frequently easier to reach than an unambitious one because an unambitious goal generates low motivational force.

> **EXAMPLE**
> Imagine an adult person who is 175 cm tall and weighs 80 kg. For this person, losing 5 kg in 3 months might be realistic. Losing 15 kg in 2 months is definitely not (or at least not healthy)
> But if you think of a 175 cm tall adult weighing 130 kg, losing 15 kg in 2 months might very well be realistic.

Now why should a goal be realistic anyway? The only reason is that by setting an ambitious, challenging and still realistic goal, you will be highly motivated to achieve it. In contrast, a too ambitious and unrealistic goal will most likely demotivate you during the process, especially if sooner or later you realize that you don't have a chance to accomplish it the way you planned it.

Timely

A goal always needs to be grounded within a timeframe, because without it there's no sense of urgency. You may want to lose 5 kg, but when do you want to lose it by? "Someday" won't work. But if you anchor it within a timeframe, "by December 2012" then you've set your unconscious mind into motion to begin working on the goal.

> **EXAMPLE**
> I want to lose 5 kg of my body weight by December 31, 2015.
> The SMART model has long since been the model for business and personal goal setting. It is a solid starting place, but there are of course other components of successful goal setting. What else might each of these five letters stand for?
> S: Beyond specific, the "S" may indicate salient, stretching and significant
> M: Beyond measurable, the "M" may indicate manageable, meaningful and meticulous.
> A: Beyond attractive, the "A" could stand for accountable, (self-)achieving and absorbing.
> R: Beyond realistic, the "R" might stand for relevant, ruthless and reflective.
> T: Beyond timely, the "T" might also indicate thorough and tangible.

Take some time and think of other synonyms that come to your mind and that speak to you. The idea is to find a suitable acronym that is easy to remember but very powerful when you follow it. Again: It should empower you, so don't settle for anything that doesn't get you excited about using it.

Conclusion: As you begin to apply all of these ideas and consistently write down and formulate your goals in a smart way, the likelihood of achieving your goals will massively increase. When you follow these guidelines, you will cultivate the attitude and capability to achieve your goals. You will even identify opportunities you might have previously overlooked that can bring you closer to your goals. Goals that had seemed impossible before will begin to be more manageable as you plan SMART goals with manageable steps. If you don't do anything else but plan your goals abiding by the SMART principles on a daily basis, you will already see your productivity soar.

But will these simple steps guarantee success at all of your goals? Certainly not.

Before we move on, write down your current TOP 5 goals, as SMART as you can.

SMART goal exercise:

A) What are your most important SMART goals for this year?

1 _____
2 _____
3 _____
4 _____
5 _____

Making a SMART MOVE: 4 MOVE rule

When reflecting about my own experience and how well I was consistently achieving my goals following the SMART formula, I had to admit to myself that I still was missing out on some of my goals. At first sight, I couldn't explain why.

So I spent some time researching and reflecting, and I encountered four vital parts that are missing in the SMART formula that are so important for achieving goals. In fact, they are even more important than the SMART goal formula we just discussed!

I also talked to a lot of clients about this phenomenon and basically everybody seemed to have had a similar experience. So what is there in addition to the valid points we discussed in the last chapter that determines our success in achieving our goals? Or in other words, what are the four main barriers stopping you from following through?

The following 4 key ideas helped me achieve a much higher success rate, so I'd like to share them with you here: M O V E.

M: Say NO to too MANY!

That's easier said than done. Saying NO sounds good. But how do you know when to say no? What are good criteria to help you to decide whether or not to reject a goal?

It might seem obvious, but having too many goals on your plate necessarily prevents you from delivering your peak performance. You can divide your attention and your energy to many different, equally important goals, but the end result is that you probably won't be able to spend enough quality time on one goal in order to deliver excellent results.

If you do prioritize your goals and you only spend your energy on the most important and urgent goals, then you might as well scrap the non-important and non-urgent goals from your list. This way, you can free up lots of mental capacity because you will no longer be distracted by goals and tasks that aren't important and urgent.

What might help you is to think about how the great Italian philosopher and economist Vilfredo Pareto would deal with it: In his famous 80:20 rule, which in the meantime has been applied to almost all areas of life, he proves that 80% of the desired results are achieved by 20% of the efforts. So what are the 80% most important goals you MUST achieve where you can easily invest 20% of your energy into? And more importantly, identify the 80% of what you need to invest to accomplish the remaining 20%. And eventually let go of these!

So learn to say NO to some of the non-important goals and focus only on your really important ones.

O: Your OWN goals

If you really want to achieve a goal, it quite simply has to be your own goal. Let's say your boss wants you to double the sales for a specific product. She tells you specifically what to do, and she gives you a SMARTly formulated goal. And let's presume it is even attractive to you because you will benefit at the end of the year from a higher bonus payment. So far, so good.

But how likely is it that you will achieve this goal as long as it is your boss's goal for you? If you are serious about achieving your goals, make sure you own them and you can fully commit to them. It makes a huge difference whether or not you can identify with that goal of double sales. In this case, you can own the goal, because you will be intrinsically motivated to achieve it. You do it for yourself, to prove you can do it.

Intrinsic motivations are much more powerful than extrinsic ones, which is why it is important for us to own our goals. When we develop goals that are based on extrinsic factors such as a salary increase, higher bonus, etc. we are much less likely to sustain motivation to pursue these goals to completion.

V: Goals need to support your VALUES

What's stopping you? Why can't you follow through on some of your goals?

Have you ever thought about the connection of your important goals and how they support or do not support your core values?

It's quite likely that after you finished reading this book, you will never again underestimate this vitally important correlation:

> The likelihood for you to achieve your goals is in direct proportion to how well these goals support your core values.

The more your goals are in line with what is really important to you (your core values) the more motivation, determination and energy you will have to follow through and even overcome potential obstacles along the way.

Chances are that some of your goals might even be in conflict with your inner values. To avoid that, check your existing goals to see whether this might be the case. And make sure that every single one of your upcoming goals supports your most important values.

Take out your TOP 8 value list now you created in chapter 1 and check all of your SMART MOVE goals to see whether they support these values.

What do you do in the case that there is a mismatch or if some goals even violate your core values? You will want to analyze those goals in greater detail:

   a. Where does this goal came from?
   b. Is it really worth pursuing if it doesn't support, or even violates my values?
   c. How could I change the SMART MOVE goal so that it supports my values?

E: EXCLUSIVE Goals

Your goals should not be in conflict with other goals from the same area of your life.

For example, if an employee has the goal to get a promotion, he will probably need to work a little more than he already does. So maybe he needs to put in 10 hours every day, rather than 9, of high quality work. He believes he can achieve his goal with this commitment.

So far, so good.

But at the same time, our employee might have a second big dream. Let's say he also wants to become a professional golfer. He already plays very well and now he sets the SMART goal for himself, to improve his game within the next 2 years.

Let's assume that he can very well become good enough to play pro golf with dedicated training. But how long would he need to practice daily, to achieve such a level? 4 to 5 hours every day! If he didn't do anything else and solely focused on that goal, he would most likely succeed.

By just looking at these 2 goals from the same area of his life together, we see immediately that there will be a time conflict. He probably won't have 15 hours a day of dedicated time for these 2 goals, considering that he will most likely have lots of other energy and time consuming goals from other areas of his live (social network, rest, family, health…)

Checklist: Have a look at your written goals now. Check, whether your goals are exclusive and whether or not they contradict each other.

Bonus E: Emotionalized

You also want to write your goals in an emotionalized, powerful way. So whenever you are reading your goals again, you evoke some positive emotions. Charge them up with energy; write them in a powerful or humorous style.

This way, your SMART MOVE goals are not only highly effective and efficient (or in other words, smart), but also written in a way that makes you smile and really want to make them happen.

Add some fun to the sometimes dull process of goal setting. And remember: To achieve your important goals is fantastic. But maybe even more fulfilling is the journey towards achieving your goal. So enjoy every step, every action you take and every decision you make on your path towards reaching your destination. And then? You pick another challenging, fulfilling goal, make a SMART MOVE and start all over again! This way, step by step you become your best self.

MOVE Summary:

I introduced these 4 barriers to successfully achieving your goals and stated it in the easy-to-remember MOVE acronym.

> **EXAMPLE**
>
> **4 MOVE Rules**
>
> | | |
> |---|---|
> | Many | Have a limited number of important goals. |
> | Own | Be sure these are your own goals. |
> | Values | Goals should support your core values. |
> | Exclusive | Goals should not conflict with other goals. |

Practice these 4 MOVE rules, and the likelihood of achieving your goals will increase dramatically.

So whenever you commit to a new goal, think about making a SMART MOVE. Those SMART MOVEs will massively increase your ability to achieve all your important goals.

Exercise: SMART MOVE goals

Now let's see how SMART your MOVEs are already when it comes to goal setting: Take 3 of your current important goals and formulate them in a SMART MOVE way. Make sure you are very specific and check your goal against the SMART MOVE formula. Only tick the box when you know your goal complies with the formula.

Example: "I want to lose weight"

This "goal" is not specific, so you would not tick off the "S" column. It also is not measurable and not terminated.

"I will weigh between 77 and 80 kg starting on November 1st 2014" is specific and measurable (if you know what your current weight is) and it is terminated.

Here's a hint: Only you can tell whether your goal really is a SMART MOVE goal. Others might help you in telling you that your goal could be more specific, measurable, doesn't seem to be realistic or isn't terminated as such. Those variables are pretty much objective and thus your friends or a qualified coach could help you with it. But all the other factors are highly subjective: whether your goal is attractive (to you), whether you have too many goals absorbing your energy, whether it is your very own intention, whether it is in line with your values, whether it is exclusive, and whether it conflicts with your other goals.

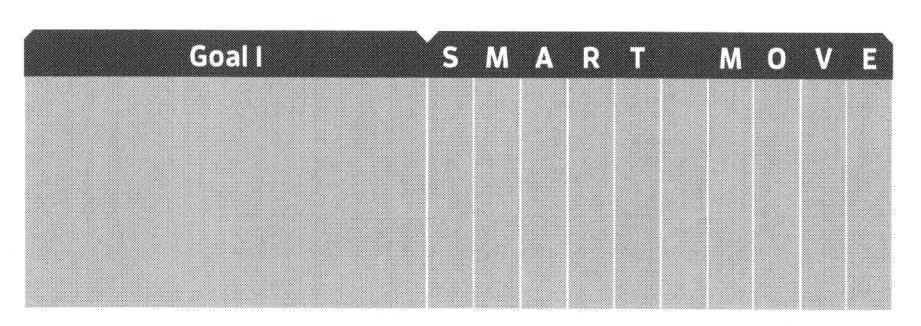

Goal I	S	M	A	R	T	M	O	V	E

Goal 2	S	M	A	R	T	M	O	V	E

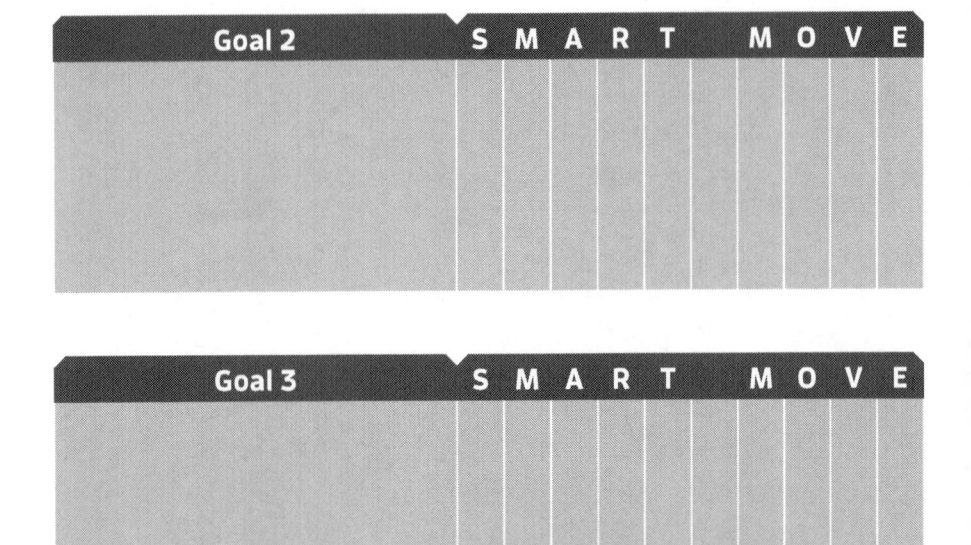

Goal 3	S	M	A	R	T	M	O	V	E

Additional goal accelerators

Having and consistently acting on SMART MOVE goals, in the order of your priority, will catapult you into the top 1% of TOP achievers.

But think about some of mankind's most remarkable inventions and achievements, both on a large scale and a personal scale:

- The invention of the automobile
- Tiger Woods decides to become the world's best golfer of all time at an all-time young age
- The US decides to send a man to the moon.

What do they have in common?

Here is JFK's famous 1962 address at Rice University on the Nation's Space Effort.

"We choose to go to the moon. We choose to go to the moon in this decade and do the other things, not because they are easy, but because they are hard, because that goal will serve to organize and measure the best of our energies and skills, because that challenge is one that we are willing to accept, one we are unwilling to postpone, and one which we intend to win...

It is for these reasons that I regard the decision last year to shift our efforts in space from low to high gear as among the most important decisions that will be made during my incumbency in the office of the Presidency.

In the last 24 hours we have seen facilities now being created for the greatest and most complex exploration in man's history.

To be sure, we are behind, and will be behind for some time in manned flight. But we do not intend to stay behind, and in this decade, we shall make up and move ahead.

The growth of our science and education will be enriched by new knowledge of our universe and environment, by new techniques of learning and mapping and observation, by new tools and computers for industry, medicine, the home as well as the school. Technical institutions, such as Rice, will reap the harvest of these gains.

To be sure, all this costs us all a good deal of money. This year's space budget is three times what it was in January 1961, and it is greater than the space budget of the previous eight years combined.

However, I think we're going to do it, and I think that we must pay what needs to be paid. I don't think we ought to waste any money, but I think we ought to do the job. And this will be done in the decade of the Sixties. It may be done while some of you are still here at school at this college and university. It will be done during the terms of office of some of the people who sit here on this platform. But it will be done. And it will be done before the end of this decade.

> Many years ago the great British explorer George Mallory, who was to die on Mount Everest, was asked why he wanted to climb it. He said, 'Because it is there'.
>
> Well, space is there, and we're going to climb it, and the moon and the planets are there, and new hopes for knowledge and peace are there. And, therefore, as we set sail we ask God's blessing on the most hazardous and dangerous and greatest adventure on which man has ever embarked.
>
> Thank you."

What do you notice? How does it highlight some of the topics we have covered so far?

Is it a SMART MOVE goal? Oh yes! Maybe it didn't seem realistic to that many people at that time. But what else do we learn about highly ambitious goals from his speech?

These goals have something more. They are ambitious, bold, courageous, extremely challenging, and emotionally charged up. The thing is, challenging goals will rev you up and improve your performance more than unambitious goals.

Challenging Goals

> "The greater danger for most of us lies not in setting our aim too high and falling short but in setting our aim too low and achieving our mark."
>
> — Michelangelo

Goals should be realistic and challenging at the same time because there are a lot of substantial positive effects that go into play the moment a goal poses a challenge for you.

1. Motivating

When you set challenging goals, it brings out your passion, excitement and enthusiasm and your likelihood of reaching the highest possible level of achievement increases significantly.

2. Encourages Resourcefulness

Every time you have a difficult and challenging goal that stands before you, chances are that you will tap into all of your resources in order for you to reach that goal. As a result, you become more creative and resourceful.

3. Personal Development

The moment you step outside of your comfort zone is the moment where your learning curve will skyrocket. Challenging goals push you beyond the thresholds of mediocrity. A challenging goal helps you to develop your talents and ability, and you increase your skills in the process.

4. Time Manager

Challenging goals force you to get organized. Most people looking to achieve a goal become better time managers. You will be getting better and better at putting together an action plan or blueprint that helps you to accomplish your goals and objectives.

If back in the 1960s, the US government had only formulated its goals based on SMART principles, then they likely would not have achieved the kind of success they did achieve. Instead they formulated their goals based on SMART MOVE principles that vastly pushed the country out of its comfort zone, and beyond what anyone had previously imagined was possible.

As you start to envision the goals that you want to set for yourself, aim to formulate goals for all aspects of your life. This will help you find balance and will enable you to pursue more goals with higher motivation. When you have a balanced set of goals, you will experience less conflict in your prioritization.

As you set goals for each area of your life, they should also be:

Self-Achievable

Good personal goals are these you can fully commit to and which are self-achievable. That means that you alone are responsible for achieving the goal. Other authors had this aspect in the original version of the SMART formula, that every goal needs to be (self-)achievable. As you have noticed, I have changed the "a" to something I regard as even more crucial to succeeding with our goals: Every goal MUST be attractive to us otherwise it won't get us going, and it won't motivate us to devote substantial energy towards the achievement.

But since it is indeed vital that we alone need to be responsible for achieving our goals and not depend on others: I have dedicated the "O" to signify "Own goals" in the 4 MOVE rules to this subject.

Positively formulated

Your goals should start with "I will…" and they must be written down!

Your brain cannot work with negative information, (i.e. input you haven't experienced). It can work only with positive information, (i.e. information from the experiences of your five senses).

Let me illustrate this with an example. If I ask you to NOT think about a pink elephant, what do you think of?

And similarly, if you set a goal like "I don't want to eat that much chocolate any longer," your brain stores this information like this: "WANT EAT MUCH CHOCOLATE."

In order to change this ineffective, negative goal into a positively formulated goal, you could say: "I will eat more organic and healthy food and give my body all the nutrition it needs."

"I am..." in the present tense

Every evening, just before you go to bed, take 3 to 5 minutes to write out your top goals for the next day in the present tense. By writing out your TOP goals at the end of each day, you will program them deep into your subconscious mind and it will help you find strategies to achieve them, even while you are asleep.

This daily goal writing will activate your mental powers. It will stimulate your mind and make you more alert. Throughout the day, you will see opportunities and possibilities to move more rapidly toward your goals.

Dump your brain!

I have mentioned several times how important it is to write down your goals, but we will explore why this is so important. Have you written down your goals in the past? Or do you still believe that it is enough to just store them in your head? Have you written down all of your goals? Or just 3 or 4 important ones? Where did you write them? Post-its, sheets of paper, a notebook, a planner, a word processor, a specific software program? A mixture of all of these?

Lee Iacocca has a great quote on the importance of writing down our goals: "The discipline of writing something down is the first step toward making it happen." By writing down your goal, you commit yourself to accomplishing the goal. It is much more powerful to actually write down your goal as opposed to storing your goal as a thought. When you write down a goal, you are promising to dedicate yourself to achieving your goal and to monitor progress towards this goal. You also need to free your mind from the responsibility of remembering your goals, and allow it to use its full capacity to actually achieve what you want in life.

Think about your mind and how it processes information. It's very similar to how a personal computer stores information in its RAM for fast access to it. But what happens if the RAM of your computer already has filled 3.9 of the 4 GB total memory? It significantly slows down the system. And to speed it up again and free up these scarce RAM resources, you have to close programs.

The same is true for your mind when it is filled to capacity with more or less useful "programs," plus information that it keeps available for you. You can take this simple test to illustrate that:

Make a simple shopping list with some grocery items. Let's say you want to buy:

2 liter fresh 1.5% milk, 250 g honey, 5 bell peppers, 1000 g fresh bread, 2 cucumbers, local newspaper, a six pack beer, 500 g organic butter.

Unless you are skilled in Mnemo techniques, you will probably have to concentrate a lot NOT to forget these simple items or to mix them up. On your way to the supermarket, could you even make a telephone call to someone without forgetting half of your list?

The obvious solution for your grocery dilemma is to simply write a shopping list, right? Because then, you can forget about all these items and focus on something else, because you can rely on your list once you are in the grocery store.

If this is logical, why do so few people actually write down their way more important goals?

Here are a few tips:

- Always take a little notebook and a pen with you to write down all ideas you come up with right away (alternatively, use a smartphone to do that).

- Have a notebook next to your bed to store ideas just before you fall asleep or if you wake up during the night.

If you like to use your brain's full capacity, make sure you first dump all of the information that is not 100% supportive to the one task you want to deal with right now on to a piece of paper or an electronic device.

How to eat that elephant? (Chunking)

Chunking is probably one of the most powerful skills with regard to goal setting and achieving at our disposal. For many people, chunking a larger goal or even a grand vision into bite-sized, manageable entries is necessary to even get started. They might appreciate imagining the bigger picture, but they need concrete, smaller and manageable sub-tasks to achieve progress on the way. If I set the goal to build a house from scratch within 2 months, most of my readers will start laughing and say, "Yeah, sure. Dream on." Because in order to achieve this goal, many, many action steps are necessary. But if the 238th action step is to select between 5 possible window alternatives and order the one I like the most considering the price, it becomes a more manageable task, right? So we can chunk down visions into many goals, and goals into many action steps.

For other people, the opposite is the right approach. They want to see the big picture first and understand the implications of their goals. You don't want to bother such a person with too many details on how to select the right windows for their house. Instead, those people appreciate viewing many parts at once so that they can understand the **WHY** easier and faster. Once they are able to understand the overall picture, they are happy to make decisions without feeling overwhelmed by too many details.

Thus, depending on the situation, it is a great skill to chunk-up or chunk-down a goal or a vision in a way that best suits our personal preferences.

Anticipate obstacles

Just briefly think about some obstacles that might come up on your way towards achieving your goal. Spending 5 minutes per goal with this exercise might be a very good investment of your time. This way, you can't go too much into the details, which would be counter-intuitive anyway. You also do not want to associate yourself with any of those challenges, at least not at this time, since you want to stay positive and optimistic.

Eventually you will face some obstacles and when you do, it feels much better if you saw those coming and if you then have at least an idea how to deal with them.

4
The art of goal achieving

Elegant strategies

Wheel of life

> "One man has enthusiasm for thirty minutes-another for thirty days, but it is the man who has it for thirty years who makes a success of his life."
> — Edward B. Butler

NOW THAT WE HAVE STARTED digging deeper into the science of goal setting, I deem it important to not jump right at the first important goal we can think of and do whatever it takes to manifest it. Let me suggest a more systematic approach which enables you to cover all your important areas of your life.

The wheel of life is a very powerful tool to gain a better understanding of the different important areas in your life and more importantly, to see how fulfilled you are with each of them right now.

The key here is to make an honest assessment of where you are right now. Your answers will determine the maximum speed of how fast you can or should go in your life.

Think about a car as your life. Your car has 4 wheels the shape of your own wheel of life. Even if it is not 100% round you can still make progress. But the more edges your wheel has — meaning that you have strong differences in your life areas — the bumpier the ride will become.

And for most of us, it won't be attractive to strive for a round wheel at all costs, because then we could settle for a "2" in all our areas, so we'd be equally dissatisfied.

So wait, imagine that the numbers 0-10 correlate with the maximum speed you can go in your life: 2 would mean you can drive up to 20 mph and a 10 equals 100 mph.

To determine the highest and still safe speed you can go, simply take the lowest number in your Wheel of Life. That's your current speed limit in your life!

And if you want to go faster and still be safe, you should think of increasing your satisfaction in the "weakest" life areas.

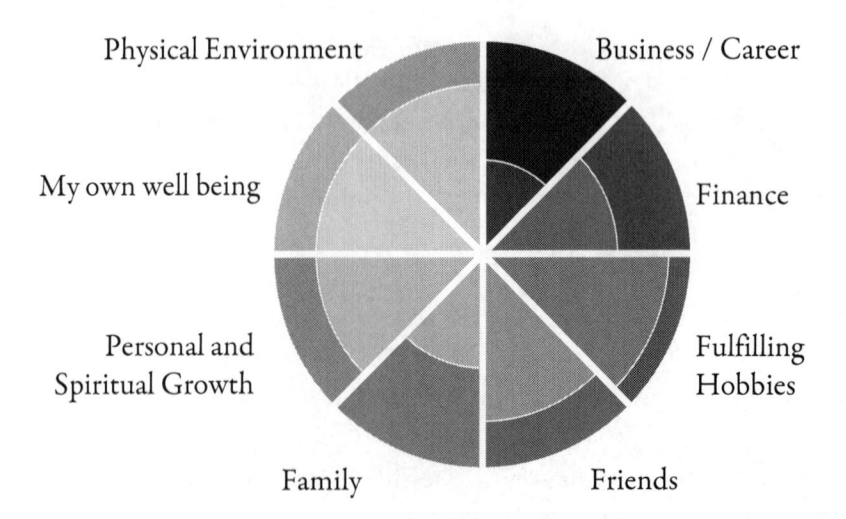

Physical Environment / Business / Career

My own well being / Finance

Personal and Spiritual Growth / Fulfilling Hobbies

Family / Friends

In the first step, think about what areas are important for you and name them. Since it will become your own wheel of life, feel free to choose vivid names that speak to you. So for example, if your family is an important area, you might choose just the name "family". Or you can come up with a creative, more charged name such as "My love life and my kids".

Once you have identified these areas — most people have between 5 and 8 main areas— you can transfer them into your wheel. Make sure each area is the same size in your wheel. Next, you will think about how satisfied you are in each of your areas at this moment. On a scale from 0 (totally frustrated or non-existent) to 10 (your absolute dream state), where are you right now?

How balanced is your Wheel of Life?

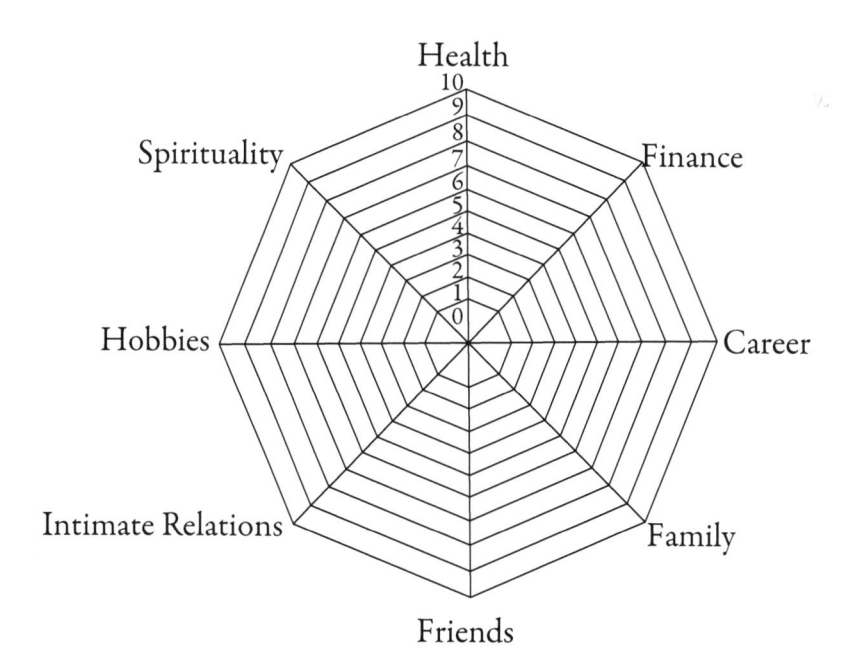

The last thing you will do to complete your personal wheel is connect the different areas. Now consider you are driving a motorcycle with your own wheel as the front wheel. Driving smoothly at about 10 mph probably would be a little bumpy, but you would do fine without crashing. Depending on the balance, you might also cruise safely at 20 mph.

But imagine, you further accelerate to 30, 40, 50, 80 mph. Is your wheel balanced enough to not crash?

How fast are you capable of driving your life?

Maybe you would even love to race at 100 mph? The whole machine is capable of this speed, if only your wheels are supporting it. So if you have a balanced wheel with 8 areas, which are each at level 3, you could safely travel at 30 mph.

If a few areas are at level 9 and 8, but only one is at level 3, you have the choice to risk speeding up to 80 or 90 mph, but with the substantial risk of crashing your machine. Or, you follow the safe route and just go 30 mph max.

Doesn't sound very convincing, eh? So you see where this is going. The area of your life with the lowest score determines your maximum safe speed.

If you want to live a charged, powered life you will want to raise your levels individually, but they should be on similar levels to avoid fatal crashes in your life.

Let me illustrate that with a personal example. When I was in my early 20s, I was on the fast track in one of my areas: I made extremely great progress in my career, had high potential, and delivered excellent results in first product management and then later in marketing & sales. When I was appointed as one of the youngest ever General Managers of a major German banking organization, I was easily at a 10 in my career field.

But of course, as with everything else, this didn't come for free. I couldn't see the costs involved for a while, but they nevertheless were substantial. While I thought that everything was going really well in my life, I was also on the fast track to burning out.

It was only later that I realized why. I was dedicating my time and energy exclusively to my career. It was no wonder I was succeeding that quickly, but not only was I not fulfilled, I was also in danger of risking my health, my relationships, etc.

So I tried to drive at 100 mph with at least 4 of my 6 life areas being between 3 and 6. It seemed to work for a while, but in the end it caused more damage than good. I neglected the importance of my physical well-being, and did not take the time to exercise and eat healthy. My friends were rightfully complaining that I almost had no time for those activities we all liked to experience together. You get the picture…

Now that you have your wonderful, unique Wheel of Life, what's next?

What can you do with this knowledge? How do you interpret it? How can you derive some goals and outcomes for your life?

Let me introduce you to a concept I call the "Peak Performance Canvas".

Peak Performance Canvas

Peak Performance Canvas
Blueprint to become your best-self

NAME DATE TIMEFRAME COACHING MORITZ OSTWALD

Hobbies & Spirituality
What do I love to do?
Where do I experience flow?
With which hobbies I feel most joyful doing them?
What is my higher purpose?

Intimate Relationships
What defines an intimate relationship for me?
Which love languages do I / my partner speak(s)?
How does my ideal mate look like?
What do I love about my partner?
What not?

Who am I?
What is my identity? What is my purpose?
What are my core values?
What are my empowering and limiting beliefs?
What are my strenghts and weaknesses?
How would my best friends describe me?
What are the things I love most?

Career
Am I passionate about what I am doing?
What do I love about my job? And what not?
If money doesn't matter, how would my dream career look like?

Health & Vitality
How healthy am I?
What does good health mean to me?
How could I improve my vitality?

Friends & Family
Who are my friends?
Why are they my friends?
What do I love about them?
What can I do to improve my friendships?

Finances
Do I exactly know how I am doing financially?
Am I satisfied with my finances?
How could I improve my situation?
What is my financial strategy?

⊖ Energy: Fears, Negativity
What drains me?
What does those changes cost me?
Who are my energy vampires?
People?
Places?
Projects?

⊕ Energy: Joy, Fulfillment
Where do I get the energy from to fulfill those changes?
What gives me joy and meaning?
What energizes me?
People?
Places?
Projects?

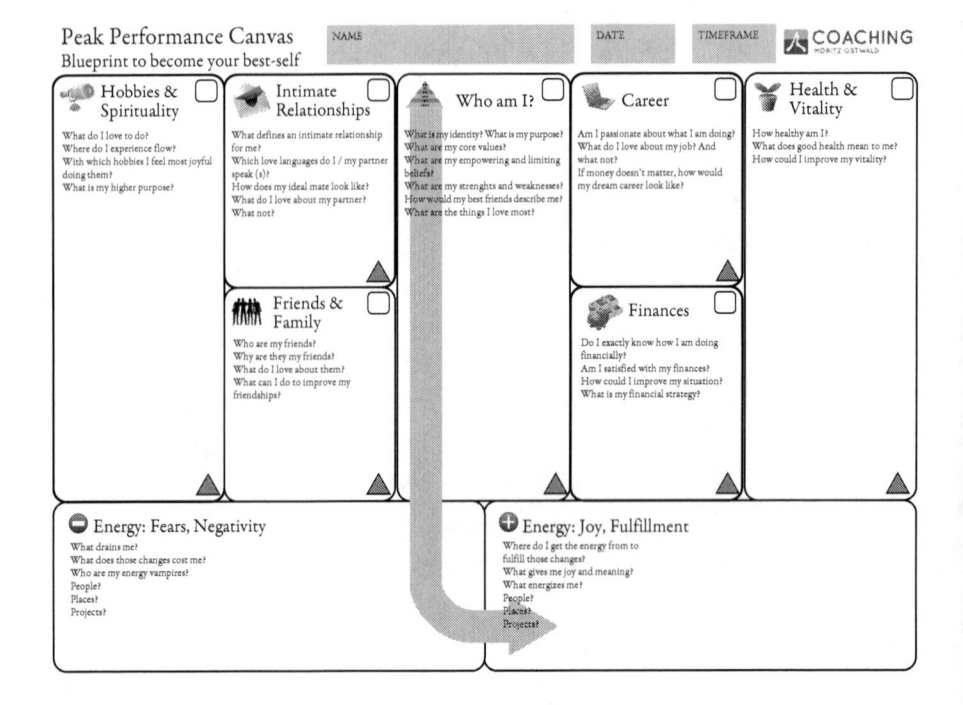

Once you have identified the important areas in your life and you assigned a score from 0-10 to each of those, you can transfer these insights into the Peak Performance Canvas. You can download a large copy of this canvas here: http://alphacoaching.co/?p=984

You eventually will need to adjust the headlines to your own wordings. For most people, the six main areas are Hobbies, Intimate Relationships, Friends & Family, Career, Finances and Health & Vitality. Those surround the middle layer: "Who am I" to which we will get in a minute.

You can now transfer the individual score you assigned for your life areas to the little box in the upper right corner. This is your status quo or how satisfied you are currently in this area. In the lower right triad you can write your desired score which you'd like to achieve within let's say 6 months. Although the temptation might be high to argue that we all would like to feel a 10/10 in all areas, we need to keep in mind that any desired change requires our attention, focus and energy. For most of us it therefore is unreasonable to aim for the "perfect 10" in all life areas, at least within a relative short time frame of 6 months.

Presuming you did not give yourself a perfect 10, you most likely already have some ideas about what you desire to be different, right? You can jot down those ideas, dreams or even concrete goals into each segment. These become the blueprint of change. The things you'd like to do or achieve so that you feel better and rate yourself higher in any given segment. Or in other words: What are you willing to do differently to become your best self?

This overview probably looks very cool now and hopefully excites you. The only remaining question is: How are we going to achieve all that?

Since we intuitively know that any of those changes don't come for free, we know that we'll have to change our habits, our behaviors, become more persistent and/or many other things. The keyword is change. We need to change something to expect a different result. And all changes cost energy. That's why so many people don't like to change. Because of the costs involved, the effort necessary can be very high.

This reminds me of Albert Einstein's famous definition of insanity: "doing the same thing over and over again and expecting different results."

Therefore the Peak Performance Canvas wouldn't be complete without a quick assessment of the resources/energy you have available for such changes. In the lower left segment, you can list all the activities, people, places, projects etc. that cost you energy. During this exercise you might identify some energy vampires which you weren't aware of but of whom you can easily let go. And thus have more energy available for your envisioned changes.

On top of that: which are the activities, people, places, projects etc that bring you joy, that make you feel good? Or in other words: Which bring you energy. Once you have identified those: Can you spend more time with them to increase your energy further?

Or in a simple sentence:
Which are the activities that drain your energy that you can let go of?

And which are the activities that empower you, which add to your energy balance?

Print out a fresh copy of your Peak Performance Canvas now and start using it. Transfer your own life areas into it together with how you currently rate your status quo. And then think about what you want to achieve, where you'd like to grow, from where you can draw energy and what you might need to let go of.

Apply your knowledge

Now it is time to make your smart move. It is one thing to read and even cognitively understand concepts and ideas. It is a complete different story to actually do and execute these new strategies so that they can become a new and empowering behavior and habit.

So please take your time and not only think about what is really important to you and to your life, but also write it down. And of course while you are at it: write those goals in a SMART MOVE way, will you?

In this next exercise, simply identify your real important outcomes per area, when you plan to achieve them, and check off any of the "SMART" boxes if they apply to the goal you just wrote down.

We will come back to your goals in later chapters and take them to an even deeper level, so make sure you devote some uninterrupted, quality time to it to get the maximum out of these exercises.

These are my **professional goals** I will achieve:

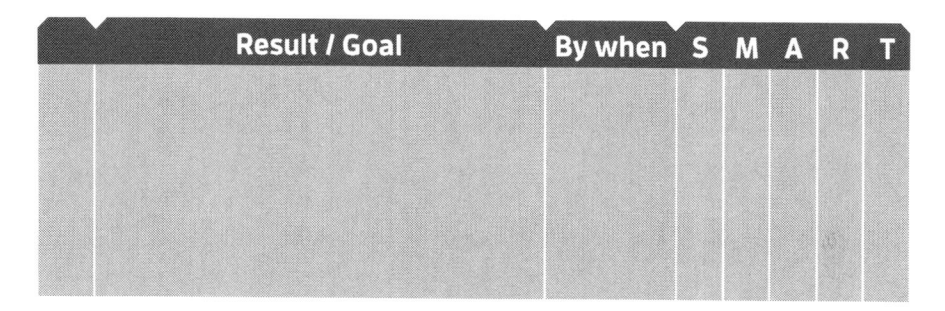

Result / Goal	By when	S	M	A	R	T

These are my **goals for friends & family** I will achieve:

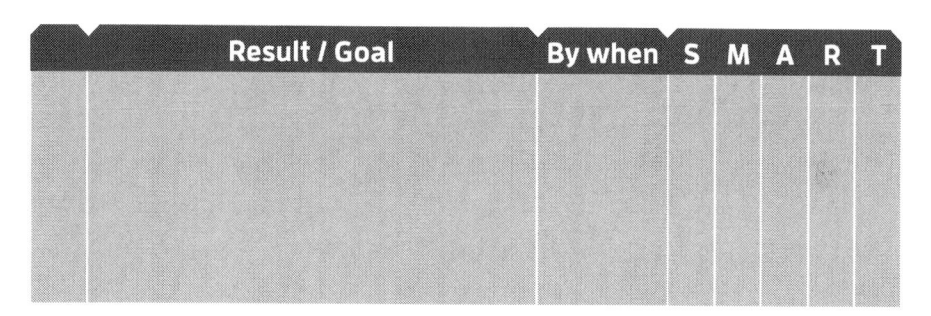

Result / Goal	By when	S	M	A	R	T

> "Friendship is a single soul dwelling in two bodies"
>
> — Aristotle

These are my **intimate relationship goals** I will achieve:

Result / Goal	By when	S	M	A	R	T

These are my **goals for health & vitality** I will achieve:

Result / Goal	By when	S	M	A	R	T

These are my **spiritual & self-development goals**:

Result / Goal	By when	S	M	A	R	T

These are my **fun goals** (hobbies, traveling…) I will achieve:

Result / Goal	By when	S	M	A	R	T

Did you find more than 1 important outcome for each of your life areas? Great! Congratulations! You really take this seriously and set yourself up for a life of meaningful success.

Now identify your number 1 most important goal per area, the one you really want and MUST achieve, and circle it in the tables above.

> "No citizen has a right to be an amateur in the matter of physical training… what a disgrace it is for a man to grow old without ever seeing the beauty and strength of which his body is capable."
> — Socrates

Goals inventory

For the case that you had some difficulties coming up with SMART MOVE goals in some of your life areas or you don't know yet how important these are for you, take the goals inventory which will help you gaining more clarity.

The Goals Inventory is a helpful way to determine which goals should take higher precedence in your life. The inventory is divided in the six main life categories, but please feel free to amend them to your very own category names. Each category has 5 questions: 2–3 pre-populated that many people have for their lives and 2–3 of your very own questions. Feel free to add as many of your own goals as you like. You rate each one on a scale of 1-5, where 5 is most important. You then examine the 5's to see which ones are actually the most important, so that at the end of the exercise you have a list of your goals in order of importance.

Take as much time to list and rate your goals as you need, but try to complete the exercise in one sitting. Try not to rate more than 2 goals per category between 4-5.

Exercise

Financial Goals	High 5	4	Med 3	2	Low 1
1. Vacation house or recreational item					
2. Improve future standard of living					
3. Ability to live off investments by age					
4.					
5.					

Hobbies	High 5	4	Med 3	2	Low 1
1. Investing more time and money in personal development					
2. Finding and pursuing one hobby that provides fulfillment					
3. Planning the next dream vacation					
4.					
5.					

Intimate Relationships	High		Med		Low
	5	4	3	2	1
1. Spending more quality time with lover					
2. Deeply understand the needs of my partner					
3.					
4.					
5.					

Friends & Family	High		Med		Low
	5	4	3	2	1
1. Education for children: college or other post-secondary training					
2. Spending more quality time with loved ones					
3.					
4.					
5.					

Career	High		Med		Low
	5	4	3	2	1
1. Make the career change towards a fulfilled profession					
2. Following through on own business idea					
3. Climbing the corporate career ladder					
4.					
5.					

Health & Vitality	High		Med		Low
	5	4	3	2	1
1. Get rid of ill habits (smoking, alcohol, chocolate etc.)					
2. Exercising regularly and feeling strong and vital					
3. Changing diet to support vitality					
4.					
5.					

Feel free to adapt the category names to your liking.

Ranking of your goals

Now it's time to gain more clarity on how important all your goals actually are for you right now.

This exercise will give you clarity on which of your goals really matter most to you and thus give you a clear signal on where you might want to focus your energy on first.

We already saw the importance of understanding our values and the order of importance in which we value them. Similarly, not all your SMART MOVE goals are equally important. By now, you will hopefully only have important goals left on your list, right? That way you don't have to bother with these "someday maybe" ideas. But how do you know which of your important goals you should prioritize? We all know that FOCUS is key and that multitasking (at least for us humans) is an urban myth! So if we really want to achieve our goals effectively (doing the right things) and efficiently (doing things right), we need to focus on one task of one goal at a time. So where do we start?

One very powerful exercise to determine your most important goals is as follows:

First, you will write your goals for the next 2 years. Start with your TOP 10 goals. Then, for each goal think about the questions:

   a. Would you still want to achieve this goal if you had only one day left to work on it before you went away for one week?
   b. Would you still want to achieve this goal if beginning next Wednesday, you're away for 4 weeks?
   c. Would you still want to achieve this goal if in 4 weeks, you're away for one year?
   d. Would you still want to achieve this goal if your doctor told you that you'll only live another year?

Exercise

	Goals for the next 2 Years	A	B	C	D
1					
2					
3					
4					
5					
6					
7					
8					
9					
10					

- A   One week away, only one day time
- B   Beginning Wednesday, you're away for 4 weeks
- C   In 4 weeks, you're away for one year
- D   Your doctor said, you'll only live another year

Interesting results, eh?

Now start with the last question: What does it tell you? If you no longer care about some of your "important" goals if you only had a year left, they are simply not important enough! So you can safely rank them lower. How about your answers to question C? Which of your goals would you want to pursue if you only have 4 weeks before you couldn't work on them for 1 year?

So you see the logic in this exercise. Those of your goals for which you clearly shouted a strong "YES" for each of the questions are your really important goals and should be on top of your goal priority.

Defer It!

Some of our dreams and wishes are nice to have and we think of them every now and then. However, they are not very important and also not urgent. So what should we do with them?

Let me recommend creating a cool new list. Yes, a list! The Someday-Maybe list. On this list, we don't need to be specific, SMART or think too much. We can simply add some of our dreams and wishes on this list to not lose those thoughts. And once every couple of months we might want to review this list as our priorities will change. Perhaps, our desire to experience one of those dreams will eventually increase. We then can simply move it from this list and put it into our DATA Plan which we will start using later in this chapter.

Growth is a good thing, or is it?

> "Life is growth. If we stop growing, technically and spiritually, we are as good as dead."
> — Morihei Ueshiba

Life is growth. I fully agree. But as with everything in life, it's a bit more complex than that. The question we should ask is not whether or not to grow. This is pretty obvious.

The real interesting question we should ask ourselves is: How much do I want to grow in each area of my life and how fast?

Growing is a good thing but we should be aware of the costs involved. Learning and growing always means investing a certain amount of focus and energy. And once we decide in which areas we want to grow and thus invest our energy into them, we also should be aware which other areas we won't have as much time for.

I therefore developed a model which I call the "Optimal Growth Strategy" which is based on the Wheel of Life and therefore reflects all important areas of our lives.

Way too many people follow this typical "Growth" cycle:

1. Identifying a deficit or pain of not being good enough or not having enough in one area
2. Feeling the need to close this gap between the status quo and the desired state as soon as possible
3. Focusing solely on improving in this one area

There are lots of disadvantages of this approach. Following this approach means the person invests their complete energy in one task, often wants to grow too quickly and thus "overdoes" it. There's of course nothing wrong with having ambitious goals but it's a thin line between become too greedy and slipping too easily into the distress zone with all its drawbacks.

Another issue is that there is certainly less energy available for all other goals and tasks from the different life areas.

How can we best grow? How can we grow at a high but sustainable pace?

We already discussed that the one extreme of not growing at all is not an option for most of us, as it equals staying in the Comfort Zone, resting and ultimately dying.

On the other hand, the other extreme is growing at all costs and often growing too fast. In the short term you might not even notice the costs and disadvantages. Working an extra 10 hours a week on top of the 50 hours you already spend on your career might not make that huge a difference in your life in that moment. But I'm sure you are very aware of the long-term consequences of focusing too much on one dimension. Most people will feel fatigue and distress at best; and depleted, depressed and unable to continue at worst, and find themselves close to a burn-out.

Think about these examples:

> **EXAMPLE**
>
> In business: Startups that grow too quick often fail and need to file bankruptcy (their equivalent of dying), because the whole organization and management needs to grow too quickly to cater to the new, arising requirements of their stakeholders. Instead of our personal wheel of life, businesses have a similar "wheel of business" with the same basic idea: One-dimensional growth is rarely healthy and sometimes leads to even devastating consequences.

Let's take a quick detour and look at how our human muscles grow.

> **EXAMPLE**
>
> ↪ Heart-Rate: 60-70% also called the Energy Efficient or Recovery Zone
>
> Whenever you train within this zone you develop your basic endurance and aerobic capacity. Your body burns a lot of fat, you might lose weight and you allow your muscles to re-energize.
>
> ↪ Heart-Rate: 70-80% also known as the Aerobic Zone
>
> While training in this zone you will develop your cardiovascular system. In this zone your body has the highest ability to transport oxygen to and carbon dioxide away from your working muscles.
>
> ↪ Heart-Rate: 80-90%: The Anaerobic Zone
>
> Training in this zone will develop your lactic acid system. The amount of fat being utilized as the main source of energy is greatly reduced. Instead, the glycogen stored in the muscles is predominantly used. Burning glycogen produces lactic acid, which can harm your body if its amount is too high in your system.
>
> ↪ Heart-Rate: 90-100%: The Red Line Zone
>
> This zone only allows you to train for short periods of time during interval training. On the plus side, you can effectively train your fast-twitch muscle fibers and thus develop speed. But if you reside for too long in this zone, you'll not only massively increase your body's lactic acid, your body will also start burning protein.
>
> The most effective muscle growth is achieved in the aerobic training zone at 70-80% of the maximum heart rate.

Although we shouldn't make the mistake of drawing a direct comparison to muscle growth and a healthy and sustainable model for our personal growth, there are a lot of good distinctions we can learn from those areas and transfer them into our "Optimal Growth Strategy".

Optimal Growth Strategy

> "When things stop growing, they begin to die."
> — Charles Gow

Let's have look at the 3 zones we can operate in:

1. Comfort Zone: <70%
2. Stretch Zone: Eu-Stress Zone: 70-90%
3. Distress Zone: >90%

Comfort Zone

As we have seen, when we talk about growth there's never much of a benefit to report while someone resides in his or her Comfort Zone. The comfort zone is a great thing: to relax and rejuvenate and re-charge your batteries. But it certainly doesn't help to actually grow our muscles, skills and virtues.

In our heart rate analogy, being in this zone correlates with a heart rate of less than 70%. If someone trains at 60% or less of his maximum heart rate, there won't even be a sufficient stimulus for any muscle to grow.

So similarly, physical muscle or personal growth won't happen in the comfort zone.

> "Life begins outside the comfort zone."
> — Anthony Robbins

Stretch-Zone

The stretch-zone correlates with a max heart rate between 70% and 90%. Similar to the physical training which is best achieved in this corridor, your personal growth and development is also best achieved in an environment that gets you outside of your comfort zone, but does not stress you too much.

For optimal, and even more importantly, sustainable growth of your skills, you want to make sure that you set goals for yourself that are in your personal stretch zone.

Just like with the growth of our muscles, learning doesn't happen during an exercise or activity, but afterwards in the recovery phase! Therefore, we need to take breaks, have a good rest and take time off to relax to actually accelerate our growth, which might sound counterintuitive for some.

Distress Zone

The distress zone is pretty self-explanatory. You'll quickly get into this area whenever you face a new scenario, project or situation, where you have never been before and you basically don't have even a clue how to act and what to do. Usually this is combined with high (external) pressure and a sense of urgency.

Residing in this zone makes you feel stressed. Or to be more precise, you will feel the negative dis-stress. Just like your body during very tough physical exercise, your mind will feel overwhelmed, you'll quickly feel fatigued, and usually can't stay too long in this zone without harming your vital systems.

In this distress zone, your body is usually quick to tell you with physical pain that it has had enough and needs a break. For our mental and cognitive growth, we need to listen more carefully to what our body is saying. Do we feel headaches, neck pain…? Do we have the urge to drink alcoholic beverages or eat chocolate?

We can learn to identify and react to more subtle emotions and reactions, which is a better strategy than waiting for serious events to happen, such as developing burn-out symptoms, heart attacks, etc.

In order to follow an optimal growth strategy, you should learn to carefully watch for any signs that you are drifting into the distressed zone. And if so, quickly and firmly readjust what you do and get yourself back into the stretch zone.

How can we use these distinctions in our planning?

A tendency many people have is to rush through to the finish line as quickly as possible, pursuing one result at all costs and neglecting other important life categories. If you only focus energy on career development, you eventually will progress there, but at the cost of ignoring other vital areas such as health or relationships.

Every action we take and every decision we make comes at the cost of a certain amount of energy, time and focus we need to invest in order to make it happen. This same energy then is obviously no longer available for other tasks.

To avoid running "blindly" in one direction and putting all your effort into one single goal, let me suggest taking a step back for a moment to also define 2 or 3 other very important goals for each of our life categories. This way, we'll quickly see that we'll need a lot of (more) energy to accomplish all of our desired goals at the same time. Or less politely formulated: It is highly unrealistic and naïve to believe that you can just add 8 more outcomes and achieve all of them simultaneously on top of your previous tasks and responsibilities.

My suggestion here is to first be conscious about those facts and then reasonably define stretch goals which motivate you and energize you, but without stressing you too much.

From my experience and as a rule of thumb, on that 0-10 scale people can manage 1 to 2 points higher in each category for a 12-month period. It is reasonable to state goals that will increase your perceived satisfaction by 1 or 2 notches each, provided that you are fully committed to those goals and make great efforts to achieve them.

If you want to focus on one category in particular and raise those levels quicker, be mindful that in the short-term you might experience a decrease of satisfaction in other categories, simply because you won't be able to devote the amount of energy and time needed for the current level.

The graphic below gives you an example.

Where is your Strech-Zone for optimal growth?
November 2014

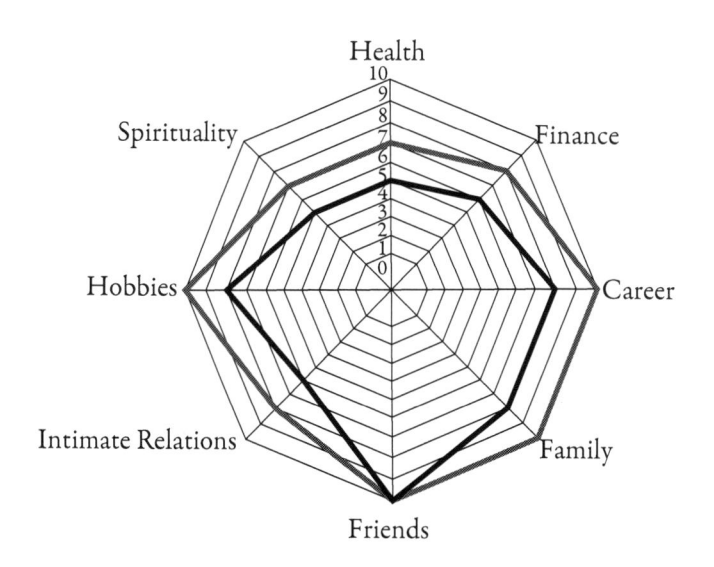

Example of an Optimal-Growth Wheel

Your Optimal Growth Wheel

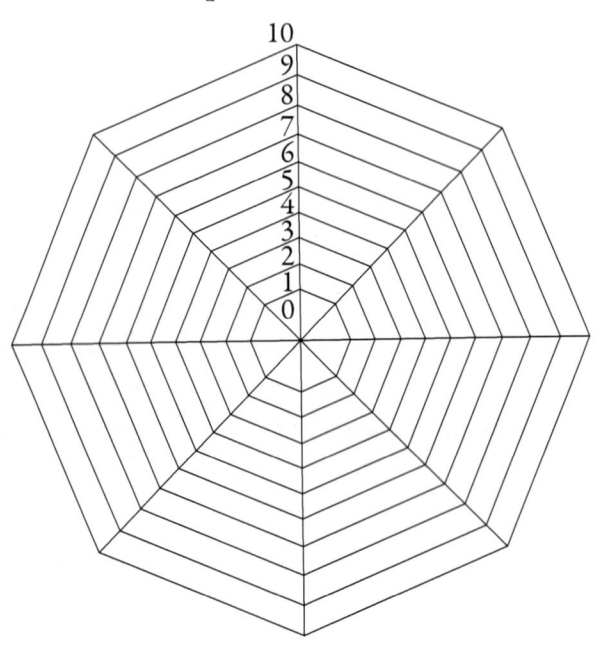

Optimal Growth Exercise

> "Do one thing every day that scares you."
>
> — Eleanor Roosevelt

Step 1: Status Quo

Any time we want to grow, make progress or simply change anything in our lives, we first need to know the status quo. Where are we honestly in any given area of our lives?

As a start, take your own categories from the Wheel of Life exercise and transfer them to the new optimal-growth wheel on this page.

Then draw the line and connect the dots of your current values you determined in your wheel of life exercise.

This inner web you now see is your current base level or in other words: Anything within this web is within your comfort zone.

Step 2: Where to grow and why

If you read this book from the beginning you should have no issues with answering these pre-requisite questions now: In which area of your life do you want to grow? And even more important: Why?

Your area of growth	Why do you want to grow and MUST grow here?

If in the very likely case that you belong to the group of achievers and you'd preferably like to improve all of those areas at the same time: Which two of those do you want to focus on first?

Once you have precise answers to these Why and What questions, you can proceed to the next level:

Step 3: Think Big

Now it is time for a great little exercise where you are not only allowed to think big, but I encourage you to become very creative and resourceful and think about the ultimate vision for each of your important life categories!

What is your ultimate outcome? Where would you ideally want to be in 5, 10 or 20 years? What would a "perfect 10" look like? What would make you and your family extremely proud if you'd already achieved it? If money and time don't matter: What would you ultimately love to do?

Take your time and craft a short vision statement for each of your life categories.

Your area of growth	Your VISION statement

How did you like this little exercise? The more compelling your vision statements are for you the more magnetic power they will hold and attract the necessary actions to materialize them. Never under estimate the power of a strong vision.

Step 4: +2 if you like it

How do you get from your Comfort Zone level into your Stretch-Zone?

In this step you'll identify ways to grow and improve your areas, step by step, expanding your current comfort zone by temporarily tapping into your stretch-zone.

Why step by step and not a massive shift in those areas where you are dissatisfied? Simply because of the energy level you'll need to invest into any of those changes. Be aware that you only have a set amount of time and energy available which you can chose to invest in any area you like. Before you commit yourself to a massive change in your life, think of the costs involved and the energy and time that consequently won't be available in other areas of your life.

Here are a few tips to avoid getting frustrated or even burned-out: Avoid getting into the Distress Zone (for too long)

How? By NOT taking shortcuts in growth by directly aiming for the maximum; instead, set challenges with reasonable growth goals within the Stretch-Zone.

Consider your individual Stretch-Zone about 2 points higher than your current Comfort-Zone. These 2 points aren't scientific but rather reflect the experience I gained with working with many clients. 1 point more is often barely noticeable, but 3 points higher is often so significant (and desirable) that some serious thought, energy and time need to be invested to achieve it… often at the expense of other important life areas.

If we aim to expand our Comfort-Zone by a maximum of +2 in our important life areas, we maximize our growth potential without getting exhausted, without risking serious damage/illness and without jeopardizing our other life areas!

I suggest that you start with this +2 idea and see how it works out for you. You can always adapt this number so it suits your needs. Just always remind yourself to see the big picture, holistically and with an open mind before you proceed with bold decisions.

Think about how our muscles work: If we train any of our muscles too hard and for too long, we slip into the anaerobic zone. This equals the Distress Zone, which causes lots of stress for the muscles and quickly exhausts them. The same is true when we reside too long in our Distress Zone: our mental muscles will get weary and as a consequence we might develop symptoms of tiredness, tenseness, all kind of illnesses etc.

A much more sustainable and intelligent way of growing is to train your physical and mental muscles in the aerobic zone at about 70-80% of your capacity.

This also correlates nicely with Pareto's 80/20 formula: Achieving 80% success/growth with 20% of the effort. You should also be aware that although the level of energy that you can invest can increase or decrease over time, generally it is relatively constant in the short-term.

Here's a simple example:

Consider the following: Your current energy level is 100%, which is the baseline of how much energy you can invest in any one of these 3Ps: People, Places, Projects.

Ask yourself how much of this 100% of your energy you are investing in each of your personal life areas.

If you want to increase and improve your situation in one area (i.e. you'd like to boost your Finance from a current 5 to a 7) you'll most certainly invest more energy in this area.

From the 100% energy you have available every day, a higher percentage is now devoted to your new goal in the "Finance" area. Be aware that this also means that there is necessarily less energy available for your other goals and tasks.

You need to ask these questions: How much energy am I willing to invest into this new goal? What are the opportunity costs? How much less energy will I have available for other projects?

To achieve a sustainable growth in your important life areas, it is recommended you:

    a. Become crystal clear on your own vision for your whole life, including specific goals and outcomes for every single life area.
    b. Set challenging but achievable Stretch-Goals for all your life areas and avoid getting into your Distress Zone. Prioritize which areas you'll focus on first and thus invest more energy.
    c. Review how you are doing once a week and adjust your actions if necessary. Repeat your self-assessment of the Optimal Growth Wheel.

Growth vs. Stress

> "To hell with circumstances. I create opportunities."
> — Bruce Lee

What is the alternative to growing? To not grow, to stagnate, to settle for less. While this alternative seems to be attractive to some people, it is certainly not for you or me ... or the human species in general. For most people, resting for too long and having no ambitious goals causes stress. But having too ambitious goals can also cause stress.

Most people do not distinguish between different types of stress. For them, any stress is bad and they try to avoid it. It's important to remember that there is no one situation, event or circumstance which is bad or stressful per se; it always depends on our perception, and the same is true for how we perceive stress.

For example, our boss giving us a deadline for a new project next Friday can either arouse Distress or Eustress. It either scares and frightens us or excites us and gets us going. Our reaction depends a lot on how we perceive this situation or in other words: What kind of belief-system do we apply for this situation. For this example, if we have a lot of (hidden) limiting beliefs about our capabilities and skills, the degree of difficulty, the relative short time etc. then we tend to experience the negative and harmful form of stress and distress, and thus feel disempowered, unmotivated and scared to accomplish the deadline.

In contrast, if we have empowering beliefs running us, we feel confident, challenged, excited to meet this deadline, to shine and be our best. In short, we still feel stressed, but this positive Eustress is totally different and we feel empowered, uplifted and can't wait to get to work.

To do or not to do: that's the question

Do you still organize your day or even your life with to-do lists? If you do, don't feel ashamed; we all do that at certain stages of our lives. But before I tell you how unproductive and unhealthy this behavior is, ask yourself these questions:

How happy are you with these to-do lists? How well have they helped you to get on top of your important life aspects? How many of those lists are spread across your office, your home, your computer? And how happy are you at the end of the day, when surprise, you not only were able to tick off all the tasks for that day, but it seems that your list now is longer than in the morning!

To-do lists are not only very unproductive since they offer you no structure, no urgency, no hierarchy and actually no good reason why you should perform those tasks.

They are in fact unhealthy as well. Because you too easily get lost in the details of those tasks and what seems to become your daily goal is simply to tick off as many as you can. Even if you do not add any new items during a day, the likelihood that you feel relaxed and fulfilled at the end of your day is very slim. Often, you feel exactly the opposite, right?

In a moment, we will talk about much better alternatives. I'll introduce you to powerful life-planning strategies in contrast to the ineffective to-do lists. But even for those few of you who pretend to be happy with your current list, consider this:

Get rid of unnecessary to-do tasks:

Vilfredo Pareto is famous for coining the 80/20 principle that suggests that 80% of the positive results that occur come from 20% of your actions. So in order to be as efficient as possible in achieving goals, it is critical to identify which of the tasks on your list are part of that 20% that have a lot of leverage. Identify those "high-leverage" tasks and get rid of as many of those tasks that are still part of the 80% as possible. Once you start using the DATA-Plan I will explain later in this chapter, it will get much easier to identify those important tasks.

Exercise: Take out your current to-do list (or write it down below) and do only one thing. Think (and eventually think twice) about which of these tasks are crucially important for you to perform today. You will most likely identify roughly the same 20% of high-leverage tasks that Pareto suggests in his universal principle.

Task	80/20

The systematic approach

> "The ultimate measure of a man is not where he stands in moments of comfort and convenience, but where he stands at times of challenge and controversy."
> — Martin Luther King, Jr.

Now that you understand how to set effective goals, let's get into what it takes to actually follow through. Once you have your goal written down, you need to create a road map for the path that you will take in order to get to your destination. What roads will you take? Where are the potential obstacles along the way? Where might you encounter delays or obstacles? Can you plan your route to avoid these? This roadmap will be your guide to where you have to go and what you have to do to get to your destination.

There's a great quote by Stephen Covey that explains the importance of this step in achieving your goal: "All things are created twice. There's a mental or first creation, and a physical or second creation of all things. You have to make sure that the blueprint, the first creation, is really what you want, that you've thought everything through. Then you put it into bricks and mortar. Each day you go to the construction shed and pull out the blueprint to get marching orders for the day. You begin with the end in mind." This mapping stage is an absolutely essential stage if we are to arrive at our final destination.

To Do Lists

Now let's move from the grand planning phase to the day-to-day tools that will help you progress in your journey and not lose track of what needs to be done.

First up: To-Do lists. They won't change your life or achieve your goals for you, but they will ensure that you won't forget vital steps on your list.

Although it is difficult to determine exactly where the simple to-do list has its origin, it is safe to assume that Benjamin Franklin was among the first to intensely use those lists for his own self-improvement. He famously detailed a thirteen-week plan to practice important virtues such as cleanliness, temperance, etc. He even tracked his progress daily on a chart.

Mr. Franklin also set himself a strict daily routine, which included time for sleeping, meals and working, all set for specific times of the day. Unfortunately, the demands of his printing business made it difficult for him to always stick to his routine.

Or take the interesting story of Charles M. Schwab, who 100 years ago, was the President of the famous Bethlehem Steel company.

At one point he felt that operations at his company could be smoother and more efficient. He sought the help of Ivy Lee, an expert in efficiency, to improve operations at his company.

Charles Schwab inquired how much Mr. Lee would charge for his guidance, and Lee said there would be no charge unless his plan worked after three months. At the end of that time, Mr. Lee asked that Schwab send whatever he felt his service was worth.

Ivy Lee met with each member of the management team for 15 minutes, and asked them to implement the following procedures.

1. At the conclusion of each workday, write down the six most important tasks to do the following day.
2. Rank each of the 6 items in order of importance.
3. On the next day, begin work on the first item and work on it until it is finished. When that task is finished, begin work on the next task and so on.
4. When the work day is over, create a new prioritized list of six items with the incomplete tasks from the current day first on the list.
5. Follow these procedures for the next 3 months and check progress.

The management at Bethlehem Steel didn't consider this idea to be very radical or transformative, but they tried it and it did wonders for the company. In fact, 3 months later Schwab wrote Lee a $25,000 check!

So without a doubt, there are good reasons to maintain to-do lists, and it is certainly better to write the important things down than to keep your mind cluttered with your ideas.

However, we all know that the reason that you didn't go for a run today or work a little harder towards a personal goal, wasn't because it was not on your to-do list. The reason why we don't do things that lead to achieving our goals lies a little deeper.

Before we go into more details, ask yourself: How well do these kind of lists work for you? Do you achieve all your tasks on your list? And if you do: How satisfied are you at the end of the day?

For most people, maintaining a to-do list is a daunting task. More often than not, their to-do list is constantly getting longer and longer. And for every task they can proudly cross off their list, 2 new tasks appear out of the nowhere. Sound familiar?

Then there is the question of prioritization? Which tasks are important? Which are urgent? And once I know that: Which of those should I prioritize? Should I start the day with the low hanging fruits or tackle the most difficult first?

Often people tend to work on the easier tasks first. The more complex tasks remain on the list, until they get really urgent and the costs involved of not dealing with them is quickly raising. A simple way to avoid such a scenario would be to change the chunking size of a given task so that it no longer appears so overwhelming, and actually feels manageable. This strategy of the "right" chunking size doesn't really make sense to use in simple to-do lists, but is very easily implemented in more sophisticated self-management strategies.

The most important downside of using to-do lists is the lack of structure. By looking at a to-do list it's hard to see the big picture. Which tasks belong together? Is there a specific sequence or order of tasks? Is a specific task the best way to accomplish a desired outcome? What were the reasons (the WHYs) we put a task "on the list" in the first place? If an outcome changes, do we actually also alter or delete the underlying tasks?

To-Do list PRO	To-Do list CON
Will help you remember tasks on your list	Does not help you actually follow through
Will motivate you to check things off	Tends to grow longer and longer and creates distress by just looking at it
Many apps and software to maintain lists	No structure; no big picture
	Why should we work on that task anyway?
	Chunk-size sometimes inappropriate

Getting Things Done

The Getting Things Done method uses to-do lists to relieve our minds from the burden of having to remember the things on the tasks that they must complete.

Getting Things Done, or GTD, is a so-called "time-management method," described in a book of the same title by productivity consultant David Allen.

The GTD method rests on the idea of moving planned tasks and projects out of the mind by recording them externally and then breaking them into actionable work items. This allows one to focus attention on taking action on tasks, instead of on recalling them.

In Allen's book on time management, the central focus is on the priority of each task. Allen's system also focuses on controlling the tasks that you add to your plate and on maintaining perspective on six "horizons of focus". Allen draws parallels between these 6 horizons of focus and an airplane taking off, where the higher the plane gets, the broader the focus is on the big picture. In this analogy it is important to maintain adequate focus on each level (Runway, 10,000 feet, 20,000 feet and up to 50,000 feet) to maintain a balanced perspective on one's progress toward a goal.

In contrast to some theories that suggest creating top-down goals, Allen recommends the opposite because focusing on bigger picture goals is not possible if daily tasks are out of control. By managing the work day more effectively, you free up time and mental energy to move up the ladder towards bigger picture issues.

Every week it is important to review each of the 6 levels of perspective, and use the review to inform the priority level of upcoming tasks and then list each task on the appropriate list according to its level of perspective. It can also be helpful to create context lists, which help you to group similar tasks together (ie: necessary errands to do while downtown).

The core of GTD is managing information pertaining to the tasks that need to be done. Oftentimes the obstacles that slow us down come from inadequate planning at the beginning. Thus at the beginning stages of planning, it is critical to generate a sequence of actions which can be done without requiring more planning. The brain's "reminder system" usually is not sufficient to remind us to do something that needs to be done. Therefore, the context lists in GTD that contain our "next actions" act as an external support that gives us timely reminders.

GTD PRO	GTD CON
Some apps and software available	Why should we work on that task anyway?
More sophisticated than To-Do lists	Chunk-size sometimes inappropriate
	Big picture is unclear

RPM

RPM (Rapid Planning Method), originally developed by Anthony Robbins, is another approach that promises to help us achieve our goals. Whereas people who rely extensively on to-do lists or the GTD method can lose sight of the "why" behind their tasks, RPM produces excellent results by keeping the focus on the reason behind what you do and what is really important in life. When you do things merely to get them done, you drain your energy and do not make as much progress towards your important goals. While many productivity systems have you focus on what you need to do, RPM forces you to switch your focus from movement to actual progress.

There are 3 steps in RPM, which, if followed, let it qualify more as a productivity strategy than other methods.

1. What is the desired result? What is the outcome I need to achieve?
2. Before we then go any deeper with the details, we actually ask ourselves, what the purpose of this outcome is. Why do we need to achieve it?
3. Only then do we collect all the action steps necessary to achieve the outcome. Or in other words: We create a Massive Action Plan (MAP).

RPM PRO	RPM CON
Starts with the Why	Not many apps/software available
Chunks tasks together	Does not acknowledge the individual values and beliefs
Lets users calibrate with the big picture	Does not utilize the power of delegating

DATA-Plan

> "Choice: it is always your next move."
> — Napoleon Hill

Although RPM offers some unique ideas and a different focus then other more traditional planning systems, there are still some shortcomings that need to be addressed elsewhere.

After years and years of working and fighting with various derivatives of to-do lists, GTD sheets and even RPM tables, I came up with an enhanced strategy that incorporates all the vital success factors that influence our likelihood to achieve our outcomes.

I knew I needed not only answers to the Why, What and How questions of Goal setting, but my goal was also to find more leverage that increases our chances, every time. Let's start with the acronym: DATA. It stands for: Determination, Achievement, Team, Activities

Determination

Always start with the WHY. What is your determination? What's your driving force to achieve a specific goal? Why is it you MUST achieve it? What is your real motivation behind this goal?

Achievement

What is it that you want/need to achieve? What is your outcome? What exactly is your goal?

Team

Do you need to achieve this goal by yourself alone? How about finding leverage for it or for its action steps?

Activities / Action steps

What needs to be done to achieve this goal? What are the specific action steps?

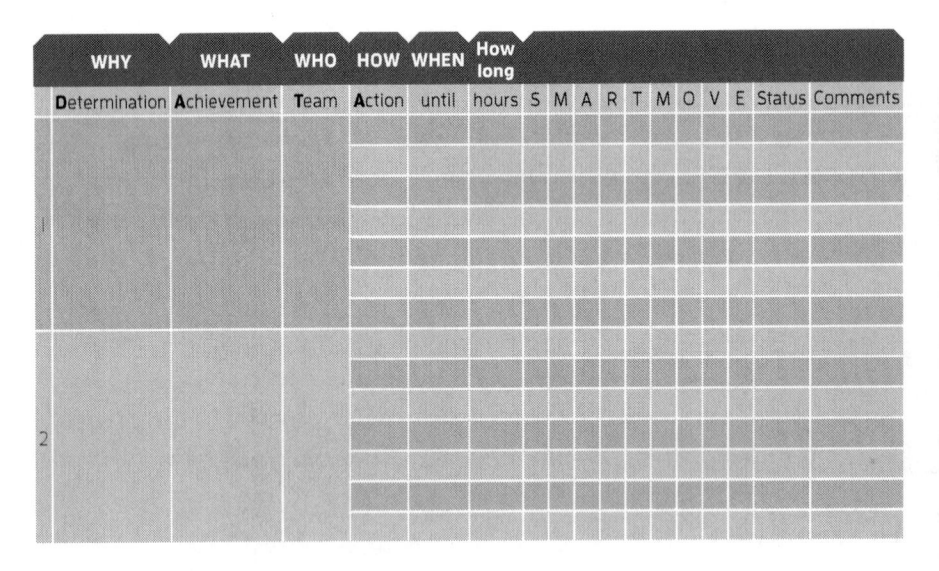

WHY	WHAT	WHO	HOW	WHEN	How long	S	M	A	R	T	M	O	V	E	Status	Comments
Determination	Achievement	Team	Action	until	hours											
1																
2																

These DATA fields are certainly the most important aspects of your goals. But as we have seen in earlier chapters, we need to ask some more questions to become crystal clear of what needs to be done, when, by whom to achieve our outcomes.

One additional layer in the DATA Plan is the "WHEN". When does a specific action step need to be completed? This information helps a lot when it comes down to organizing your schedule, when you have to decide which action steps you will work on a specific day. Not all tasks are equally urgent; some can wait because there won't be a benefit if you complete it early.

How about the importance of different activities? They should all be VERY important and absolutely vital to achieve your outcome. Always ask yourself this question first: Do I (or someone you appoint) really need to do this task? Only include an activity into your DATA Plan when the outcome would NOT be reachable without it. Think of the Pareto formula: With 20% of the tasks you'll get 80% of the results. This way you'll get rid of many unnecessary "someday-maybe" tasks.

Also, try to estimate how long a specific task will take you to complete. It is easier to determine how much some smaller chunk tasks will need then "guessing" how much time is needed for a whole project or major outcome. Once you have estimated the duration of each task, you can simply add those hours or days and receive a much more accurate figure for the parent outcome. Also, by determining the duration of an activity level, you can schedule them more accurately.

To maximize your likelihood to get your outcomes done effectively, you should check your goals and activities against the SMART MOVE formula.

Is every single action step SMART compliant? Are your tasks specific, measurable, attractive, realistic and timely? And on the level of your outcomes: Are you goals following the SMART MOVE formula?

> **EXAMPLE**
>
> Outcome: One-week vacation with your friends
>
> Let's see how this outcome can be described and detailed in the DATA Plan:
>
> 1) What is your outcome – What is the desired achievement?
>
> First, state the precise achievement, your goal. Formulate it wisely and make your SMART MOVE.
>
> Example: A 7-day golf vacation in May 2015 in the east of Mallorca together with James and Nils and their families.
>
> 2) Why are you determined to achieve it?
>
> Before you proceed with any detailed planning you want to go back to step one and ask yourself: WHY do I want and/or need to achieve this goal? Why is it important? Why MUST I get there? You always want to answer this as precisely as possible as those reasons are your driving forces to actually achieve this goal. If you have doubts or it is only nice to have, you either want to get rid of this outcome at all and don't invest your energy into it. Or, you might want to reformulate and tweak your goal until you really can't wait to get it done.
>
> Example: I love vacations; I deserve a wonderful vacation; Mallorca is one of my favorite places; May is a very good month to visit the island; I haven't spent much quality time with my dear friends recently; they love the idea as well and already came up with some great activities ...
>
> 3) Who can help you achieve it – Who is your Team?
>
> In this step think about who can eventually help you achieve this goal. For almost any major outcome there are ways other people can and will help you, if only you ask them. For many, it is a general tendency to believe, that they have to do it on their own. Some are afraid to ask others for help. Others believe that they are better capable of doing tasks themselves. To effectively delegate or assign tasks to other people is a skill which can be learned and improved like all other skills.

Example: Nils and James: They can do parts of the planning. A travel agency: Those experts can do various tasks including flight search, finding a suitable hotel and rental car or bus transfer etc.

4) How are you going to achieve it – What are your action steps?

Now finally we are down to the action level. This is the section where we will want to list every major action step which is necessary to achieve our overall goal. What a "major action step" is, is a very subjective call. Some only write those 10.000-feet tasks such as "Organize leisure activities". They have rather high chunks and are happy with them.

Other people will go much more detailed, i.e. to a 100-foot level and break it down (chunk it down), i.e.

- Call Quad-Rental Company in Palma for a 3-hour tour on Tuesday
- Sign contract with catering chef for a BBQ dinner on Wednesday

For every separate action step you can then assign somebody from your team to it. You then will think of the deadlines for every action step: when does it need to be finished?

And to be better able to schedule all of those tasks, you might also want to estimate the duration of each task. How long do you (or one of your resources) need to finish each task?

If you follow the DATA Plan Excel sheet, you then can check each task against the SMART MOVE criteria. If any task does not support one or more of those criteria, you might want to think about whether the task is really vital for the goal or whether there is another way to achieve the same result, and it can be replaced.

When you use the DATA-Plan you will also populate the "Status" columns on a regular basis. This way, you can quickly see how far you are towards any action step and your overall goal.

To print your own copies of the DATA Plan or to use it electronically, you can download it the Excel version here: http://alphacoaching.co/wp-content/uploads/DATA-Plan.xlsx

5
NOW is a good time to take actions

> "A journey of a thousand miles begins with a single step."
> — Confucius

EVEN THOUGH ALL OF THESE goal-setting strategies and tools are highly valuable, at the end of the day, the most important thing you need to do is: Take Action NOW! Take one small step towards achieving your goal today. Don't defer it.

What can you do TODAY to get closer to your goal? Maybe you make a phone call. Or you schedule a meeting. Sign up for this training. Finish reading this book…

There are basically millions of different action steps you could do. But how do you know with which one you want to start now?

Where do you start?

Never underestimate the power of your habits

> "Insane are those people, who expect different results while continuing doing the same things"
> — Albert Einstein

WHAT DO YOU EXPECT FOR your life after you have finished reading this book? Do you think the likelihood of achieving your important goals massively increases? No! It doesn't.

I will tell you a secret: You can read this book 5 times. Attend a dozen self-help seminars. Spend another $10,000 in coaching and training. And intellectually understand all of the concepts, ideas and exercises. Nothing will change in your life. Trust me, nothing!

Only in the moment you decide to actually change some of your routines, some of your habits will you start to reap the rewards. Intellectually understanding something is a prerequisite. But the applying of new habits is the key to success. Only then can you expect different and better results.

This starts already by "reading" this book. Are you the kind of reader who skims through the content, looking for one or two new ideas and for what resonates with you? Nothing wrong with that. I love speed-reading, too.

Or do you thoroughly "work" with this book, underlining new ideas and paying particular attention to the chapters which are not resonating with you in the first place? And most importantly: Do you take the time to do the various exercises? And with the answers challenge your status-quo?

You will most likely belong to the second category. If not, may I encourage you this time to make an exception to your rule and just give your best and commit yourself to "work" through all the chapters?

Habit of self-discipline

Developing and nurturing the habit of self-discipline is easily among the greatest gifts you can give to yourself. In your life, you have likely come across hundreds, if not thousands, of great pieces of advice, tips and tricks about how to live a successful and happy life. There are so many books and seminars that you have surely learned a ton of powerful strategies to improve your life.

But how many of these do you actually do on a daily basis? Do you remember the Harvard study? Everybody knows that it is beneficial to write down your goals. But only 3% do it! 3%! Those 3% actually created the habit to do so.

The same is true for most of the adults with regard to applying their knowledge to achieve their goals. Roughly 3% are following through, willing to constantly change and improve their lives, implementing new tools and strategies, evaluating them, getting rid of old tools and introducing new ones.

Guess which part of the world is regarded to be more successful, more fulfilled? Yes, of course, those 3% willing to go the extra mile to create empowering beliefs and habits that they set up for success. This of course takes a lot of self-discipline, practice and a high degree of persistence and it comes with an opportunity cost involved as there will be many things you can't do simultaneously. Or in other words and more positively formulated: which do you decide to let go. To not pursue. The Goals Inventory above gives you a very good starting point to decide on which goals you should invest your energy and focus in.

Practice visualization and anticipation

Have you ever noticed how top athletes prepare themselves mentally before they enter a competition? These days, it's no longer enough to be the physically fastest, strongest, fittest person in almost any sport. What it takes to win competitions and enter the circle of the world's best is to a high degree determined from their mental strength.

Do you remember the very impressive example in the sport of bobsleigh from the last chapter? Watch those athletes the 2 or 3 minutes before their race starts: they close their eyes and move their body and head in all kind of directions. What they are actually doing is driving down the sled, mentally, in real-time! They visualize every single curve and every challenge on their way until they cross the finish line. Or in other words: they win the race even before they started.

This technique does not only apply to athletes, determining whether they win or lose or make half a million more if they sink this next 10-foot putt. We all can make use of it for our daily lives, in sports and in achieving anything else of importance for us.

As a start, try to vividly imagine how you will feel once you have accomplished any one of your goals. Just fantasize for a moment how this would make you feel: maybe you feel proud, happy, fulfilled. Would you smile? Stand tall? Celebrate? Shout out loud? Whatever it is for you, fully associate yourself with this moment of victory and enjoy it!

This very simple technique alone will change the way you approach your goals. On top of the motivation you already had when you formulated your goal, you now have another powerful force pulling you towards it.

Review progress regularly

On your path to achieving your goals, it is important to review your progress regularly. But this does not mean you do so whenever you feel it. Remember: you can only manage what you can measure.

You have to set up times at regular frequencies to review your progress and to measure your progress towards your goals. Set up a time to review your progress at least every week. One way of doing this is to use the DATA-Plan and update the "Status" column of every action step once a week.

In addition to measuring your progress, you should also use this time to assess whether or not the goals you set still fit your values, priorities and desires. If you find that you have spent an entire year working towards a goal with little progress, you might decide to spend your time on another goal, rather than wasting your time and feeling bad about your lack of progress. Perhaps the goal is too big or it is just not as desirable as it used to be. When you are not making the progress you want to see, it is important to analyze the factors that may have led you not reaching your desired goal and take steps to overcome these challenges. If you still are not making the progress you would like to see, take active steps to ensure that you do (i.e.: hire a life coach or ask for support from family members or friends).

Make it a MUST

How often have you heard people saying: "I should do this and that." "This year, I should really stop smoking."

And you know instantly, they won't do it. Just like they haven't followed through on such goals in the past. Why is that?

The motivation for them to really go all out and make that goal happen is not high enough as long as they believe they should do it. They are not really committed. Think about your own projects. What would you do differently?

What would happen if you formulate SMART MOVE goals and instead of saying: "I really should do this now" you say in an absolute convincing, authoritative voice: "I will do it because I MUST! I won't even waste 10 seconds of my precious energy to think of excuses and how I could save face in the case I don't succeed. Because, I will succeed!"

Do you feel the difference just by reading those sentences? Once you really commit yourself fully to your important goals and you associate enough positive aspects with their achievement, once you link the pleasure of having done it plus whatever positive benefits you will enjoy with it, it becomes so much easier to follow the path towards your goal achievement.

Here's another potential reason for people who seem to not achieve their SMART MOVE goals even though they follow most of these best practices in this book.

We human beings love hearing stories. We love to follow strong leaders who tell us their stories, how they struggled in the beginning and then transformed themselves to the successful leader/celebrity/politician they are now.

Funny enough, we also like to hear stories of people who fail with their goals. Why is this? Because they make us feel better. Since most people like to compare themselves, it just feels good if somebody we know did even worse than what we did.

Here's what's interesting in connection to our ability of goal achieving: even without realizing, the majority of stories we hear every day are those we tell ourselves! Think about it: most of your thoughts you have every day are repetitive, in fact, 99% of them are the exact same you had yesterday. And the day before… And what do you do with your thoughts? You create stories around them, which you tell yourself, your friends and partners.

Those stories become your truth. You believe in them. And eventually, other people start believing in your stories as well.

As you know, there are basically just two different types of stories: empowering and dis-empowering stories. For example, is your story anything like Muhammad Ali's?

> "I am the greatest of all time!"
> — Muhammad Ali

And you tell this story over and over and over again. Guess what happens? Yes, it will become a self-fulfilling prophecy because you will direct all your energy, all your powers and focus towards this story.

Unfortunately this is also true for any dis-empowering story people might have. Whoever thinks that they don't deserve something, that they are not good enough, too young… they are exactly right. Henry Ford already knew that: "If you think you can do it. Or you think you can't. You are always right."

How can you utilize this for your daily practice? Just use this simple 3-step Muhammad Ali exercise:

1. Identify your negative stories
2. Give up these stories and replace them with a better, positive and empowering one
3. Tell this new story over and over and over again. Tell yourself, your friends, your family, the whole world (even if they don't want to know it. But hey, by now, you really shouldn't bother any longer by what other people think about you)

Accountability - Mastermind groups

> "Never doubt that a small group of thoughtful, committed citizens can change the world. Indeed, it is the only thing that ever has."
> — Margaret Mead

Another important strategy in helping you achieve your goals is sharing them with others. When you share with others your goals and your progress towards these goals, you will have a built-in added incentive to achieve them. You will also have their support and understanding, which can be absolutely essential to helping you achieve your goals.

What does this famous group of people have in common?

- Plato, Socrates, Aristotle
- Franklin, Jefferson, Washington
- Goethe, Schiller, von Humboldt

They all befriended each other and formed their own mastermind alliances. A mastermind alliance is a group of 2 or more people working together to help each other accomplish a definite end in a spirit of cooperation and harmony.

It's a term created by Napoleon Hill in his ground-breaking book, Think and Grow Rich from 1937.

There are numerous benefits of joining or creating one or more mastermind groups. So many, that you can easily fill a whole book with it. Here are the TOP 5 most important aspects and a brief explanation:

- Mutual support
- Accountability

- Differing perspectives
- Resources
- Share contacts, expertise and empowering experiences

Mutual support: Mastermind members offer themselves support where it is needed by other members. With their different perspectives, skills and experiences they are dedicated to help their peers to succeed.

Accountability: Fellow group members hold themselves accountable to goals they set. Maybe the single most powerful benefit!

Differing perspectives: Hearing the different views of fellow mastermind participants allows participants to see issues one wouldn't otherwise become aware of in life, and in the approach to reaching goals. You do not necessarily have to agree with their assessment, but it always gives you a better understanding of how you can also change your approach.

Resources: Everyone in your group will have access to a different skill-set and network of people. When you ask for help in your mastermind groups (and yes, this is the place to ask for help), these resources help you make progress in ways you never could by yourself.

Sharing: Sharing successes and challenges with like-minded people can be a very empowering experience. The more you open yourself and the more honest you are with your fellow masterminds, the more you will benefit from their empathy, their experience, their network, etc.

If you haven't experienced the magic of being part of a strong mastermind alliance, let me encourage you to create one yourself. Once you are enjoying the company of your fellow masterminds every week or twice a month, you will see how much more focused you are working towards your own goals, because they will hold you accountable for what you are planning. And trust me, you eventually fool yourself every now and then, but you wouldn't want to let down your masterminds and explain to them why you just didn't have the time, right?

Celebrate milestones

> "The more you praise and celebrate your life, the more there is in life to celebrate."
> — Oprah Winfrey

Now maybe you have just arrived at the single most important chapter of this book. And it is one of the shortest and easiest to understand. And best of all, you probably don't have to learn any new skill or technique.

"The journey is more important than reaching the goal itself."

Have fun! Enjoy the ride! Be proud! Be playful!

It is a very vital aspect of achieving your meaningful goals and every peak performer understands and follows this concept: not only to being highly disciplined and focused, but also to constantly rewarding yourself for all the efforts you make. Way too many people get stressed over their huge goals and often get lost in their busy day-to-day duties.

My question to you:

What do you like most to reward yourself? Reading a great book? Walking through the park? Playing a round of golf? Indulging in Ben & Jerry's ice cream? Think of your own TOP 5 and write them down here:

1
2
3
4
5

When you arrive at a milestone along the way, make sure to celebrate it. And with it you not only reduce your stress levels but more importantly you program your subconscious mind to crave more from these rewards. So you will naturally want to reach the next milestone of your SMART MOVE goal and celebrate again.

Rather than letting your mind be consumed with thoughts about how far you still have to go, think positively about your accomplishment, stay in the moment and concentrate only on the next action step which will lead you closer to achieve the next milestone.

Remember how you'd eat an elephant: Bite after bite. Celebrate milestones and move to the next step in your journey.

Some warnings

While setting goals is a very powerful practice that will improve your life and your success in life, when you don't really dedicate yourself to the process of effective planning and follow-through, then you will likely not achieve your goals. Even worse you might become pessimistic and waste a great deal of time and energy.

As we have seen, the key is to become aware of who you are, what you really want to achieve in your life and why that is. If you are crystal clear on those two questions, I'd bet that you are also highly motivated to create your DATA Plan and follow through.

So the following warnings will most likely not apply to you. But judge for yourself:

Unclear goals

This is probably the most common mistake people make in the whole process. Of course, you won't because you are making SMART MOVEs, right? But being unclear of what it is you want to achieve and how you are going to approach it almost always ends up in a disaster. Just think back to the times when you still weren't so sophisticated. How frustrating it was to NOT achieve your New Year's resolutions. Now you know how minimal your chances have been.

Goals and confidence

While it is highly motivating to set yourself SMART MOVE goals and to enjoy the process of getting closer to your goal, sometimes your priorities might change. You no longer feel positive and motivated to work on one of your goals.

What happens in such a common scenario? Presuming you stick to the goal, your motivation declines. With that, your perceived distress will increase. And all of a sudden, you are no longer confident and committed to achieve this goal. So what is the solution?

You should reassess your outcome. Make it a habit to get back to the drawing board every few months and review all your major goals you are currently working on. Are they still SMART MOVE goals for you? Or has something changed? Since life is all about change it is quite likely that new opportunities and challenges will arise which you want or have to give your attention to. With such a shift of your priorities, some of your goals you worked on no longer pass the SMART MOVE test. You always have the option to let go of one goal in favor of an even more desirable one. Make use of it! Don't be ashamed to stop working on certain goals in the middle of the process. Maybe it feels like a failure for you in the beginning, but trust me, it's more a feature than a bug. Because what is the alternative? To stick to your goal until the very end, but what is the price you pay even if you succeed? You'd need to invest far more energy than you originally thought. Energy, that of course isn't available for any other projects.

Or, even worse, you stick to it (maybe because of you being proud…) only to realize at the very end that you failed with it. And just imagine how that would feel and how much more energy you then would have wasted. Not to mention, what would happen to your confidence and your ego…

Missed opportunities

Once you set a clear, SMART MOVE goal, you focus your attention and effort on this single outcome. For purposes of that task, they're great, but that same focus means not giving attention and effort to other things. So you need to be aware of the big picture, of all the important areas in your life and what you'd like to do and also stop doing.

This way, there will still be literally hundreds of tempting ideas, projects and thoughts which you will not pursue and opportunities you will miss. There might even be the voice in your head questioning whether this is the right way to live your life.

But you know that once you focus your energy on a few major goals in each of your important life areas that are in line with your values, beliefs and desires, you allow yourself to enjoy the process and flourish.

Too Many Goals Make Nothing a Priority

This is very true and can be very frustrating for people, especially for those who'd consider themselves as overachievers. Do you know those people who just seem to have too many ideas and goals?

Maybe you want to help them and give them a copy of this book, since the SMART MOVE was designed to cure them. If I only came up with that formula ten years ago… how much time and energy I could have saved…

Goals intended to impress

Ah, this is a good one, too. Depending on how strong your healthy ego is, this topic might sound familiar to you. Or at least you know someone who'd qualify for this category, don't you?

Sometimes people tend to formulate goals with one clear purpose in mind: to impress their peers. And there is absolutely nothing wrong with goals that impress others. As long as they serve you and your life and are desirable for you. But sometimes you aim so unrealistically high to impress your girlfriend that you put yourself under enormous pressure. The question is: is it really worth it to look good at this moment, when you share those impressing goals with others? Maybe it is. But more often it is not.

You can ask yourself a simple question to avoid falling into this trap: if I never tell anybody about this goal, if I completely approach it in silence and just for my own pleasure, would I still have this goal and invest my precious energy into it?

Enjoy the ride

> "The future depends on what we do in the present."
> — Mahatma Gandhi

> "Life isn't about how to survive the storm, but how to dance in the rain."
> — Unknown

MAYBE THIS IS THE SINGLE most important idea you can get from this book. So let me keep it very short and sweet:

Enjoy the whole process. Have fun. It's not at all (only) about getting what you think you want and deserve. It's about aligning your whole life and every day you can spend on this planet with what is really important for you. When you do this, you will not only achieve your important outcomes but you will enjoy every aspect of it. The whole roller-coaster ride. You are here, you paid for it, so why don't you enjoy the whole thing? Embrace every aspect of the journey and play this vital game like real leaders do:

1. See it as it is but not worse
2. Envision it better than it is
3. Close the gap between 1 and 2.

Talking about enjoying the ride: In the summer of 2005, I was on a 10-day biking tour with Torsten, a good friend of mine. Our idea was to cross the Alps with our mountain bikes, starting in Neuschwanstein in Germany with a destination Lago di Garda in Italy. It was a very memorable and exciting vacation, for many reasons… especially for unexpected reasons.

One day at the end of July, we had a 40 km trip through Süd-Tirol, Austria. It was a magnificent day, 28° C and the sun was shining. After a few hours of biking through the forests and mainly uphill terrain, we passed a Sommer-Rodelbahn which basically is a track similar to a bobsleigh except that a) it's open during the summer months and you sit in a little vehicle with wheels driving down a solid concrete track and b) it is designed for kids.

There was nobody there and since we needed a quick break anyway, we decided to satisfy the little boy in us and gave it a try. The track was about 2 km long, downhill and from just looking at it I should have realized that there were some steep passages as well. But even if I would have noticed it, this thing was designed for kids, eh? So what could possibly go wrong if we drive down this track?

Torsten is 2 m high and weighs a bit more than I do. He decided to grab a vehicle and drive down first. Being in a very playful mood anyway that day, I made my decision to "catch" him on this single track or at least get very close to him. I started about 10 seconds later.

To defy the odds and catch him, I knew I would need to alter the only variable we both had to control the vehicle: there was a huge "lever" which we could press down to activate the brakes. That was it. So I knew to overcome the laws of physics and cruise down at a higher speed, I'd need to take some risk and brake later than I thought he would do; after all I then would be a bit more aggressive before the turns and be able to catch up with him shortly.

How I loved my master plan! Only it didn't take long to understand that "knowing the path is not walking the path". After 5 seconds I already had a good speed and really enjoyed this experience. The first 3 turns came and I rushed through them. My adrenalin was rising and I felt like a 12-year-old boy again. I hadn't made use of the brakes yet so I was pretty sure my plan was brilliant and I would shortly be able to see my friend.

Then, there was the next turn coming. This one was different, it was way higher and steeper and I wondered for a moment if I should slow down. But knowing my outcome-to catch up with Torsten- and also relying on the good Austrian engineering and the fact that kids drive down this track every day, meaning it needed to be very safe, I didn't brake.

The next 10 seconds or so felt like an eternity, especially from that split second when my vehicle fell over and I was catapulted out of the car and literally slid over the concrete on my bare arms and legs until I finally stopped on the right. The first shock vanished rather quickly, but what remained were my 3 and 4 cm large open wounds on my legs after my skin burned from sliding on the concrete at high speeds. The pain was pretty substantial but bearable. When I finally walked down the rest of the track, my arms and legs were bleeding, but I managed to keep smiling because I obviously didn't want to look too stupid when I encountered my friend again. I guess I failed also with this idea as he started to laugh uncontrollably once he saw me. When I explained to him that those wounds really hurt and asked him to find a first-aid kit, he walked away and came back 5 minutes later.

Now this might be a painful and/or entertaining story, depending on which angle you look at it from. But the real story, the real experience happened in these 5 minutes I was there on my own.

5 minutes that changed my life. What I didn't see initially was that in fact I wasn't alone at the exit of this amusement park. About 20 meters away, there was an old man in his 80s standing and looking at me. He slowly approached me and asked how I were doing.

"Well, thanks for asking but you must have seen what just happened and that I'm bleeding everywhere."

"Does it hurt?" he replied. I wasn't sure whether he was making fun of me as well, since he looked very serious and yet relaxed. After I promised him that it really, really hurt he went on:

"Good, Congratulations." I really didn't know what to think or how to react to the fact that I felt like he had just insulted me. It turned out that I didn't need to think anything, but just listen to what he then told me.

"You know," he started, "I can imagine that you feel the pain right now. But this is a good thing. And honestly, I envy you. And I'd swap with you right away."

"But Sir," I replied, "with all due respect, this really hurts a lot and why would you possibly want to change with me?"

"Well, when I was your age, I had huge dreams and fantasies of what I wanted to do with my life and who I wanted to be. I loved my dreams and they gave me a lot of energy. But the times were different. It was shortly after the war and I was lucky enough to have a decent job in the heavy-industry that made me enough money to pay my rent and buy some food. We did not have many days of vacation per year and even during those days, I worked for other people to make some more money. This cycle of working hard and dutifully, then resting a bit and starting all over again went on for many years. My dreams were still present and I told myself that I would fulfill them in a couple of years, when I had the money and the time. After roughly 20 years I realized that the day that I would have enough money to buy the beautiful convertible car I dreamt of and when I would have 4 or more weeks to travel around the world wouldn't possibly come until I retired. So I altered my dreams in a way that I visualized exactly how I'd feel this day when I turned 65 years old and retired: all the freedom to do whatever I wanted to do and enough money to afford the journeys. Nothing unreasonable, but those dreams kept me going and gave me so much meaning."

I was listening tentatively to his story, almost in a trance state, and I felt that what he shared with this stranger, me, couldn't be a coincidence, but that if I continued to listen to his wise words I could gain a very valuable lesson here.

So I encouraged him: "And, what happened then?"

"Well, when the day of my retirement, the day I was living my whole life for, finally came, I had a sudden eureka moment. I realized that indeed I was a free man now. I had all the time in the world to travel wherever I wanted. I had enough money to buy some nice things for myself, and it was even enough to afford my BMW convertible."

"This is wonderful," I replied.

"But something else happened in these first days: something very unexpected and something I wasn't prepared for during my whole life. When I test drove this dream-car, a drive I had visualized a thousand times and how it would make me feel… I felt nothing. There was a huge void which I barely can explain. It just felt so unimportant, so empty. It was a huge disappointment.

"So I didn't buy this car. And worse: I also didn't go on any longer trips and I also did not travel around the world. Because I simply realized that my priorities had changed. My desire for what I thought would fulfill me was gone.

"I realized that I didn't pursue the wrong dreams but rather fooled myself that one day into thinking that everything would be different and fall into place, that one day the time would be right. Except that this one day never came. This was the ultimate pain.

"Maybe you now understand why I'd love to have your physical pain right now if I could also experience your freedom and joy and the excitement you must have during such a trip."

Now, I was in tears, not because of my pain, which I barely noticed any longer in this moment, but because of how his story was touching me. I had just witnessed one of the most intense and valuable 5-minute lesson of my life.

What if life ultimately really isn't about achieving our outcomes? And not even our dreams and desires? What if life is about how well we can learn to appreciate and embrace the journey we are on, our unique journey?

This gentleman taught me the real power of now. Being present, alive and "just" witnessing what is. Yes, I had physical pain. And yes, even almost 10 years later I still have those souvenirs in the form of scars. But the truth is that I knew in that very moment how happy and wealthy I truly was and that the momentary pain would make room for a far greater and more significant experience that altered my perspective on how I look at events.

In short: I learned this day that I can allow myself to enjoy the ride. Even or because of the many unforeseeable obstacles and turns which we are all facing in our lives.

How does this personal anecdote relate to the theme of this book? Does this mean we shouldn't bother with dreaming, planning, or envisioning any longer?

Quite the opposite! Knowing who we are, what we value most in life, what our beliefs are and in which direction we want to head, is crucial for a fulfilled and meaningful life. But all this won't make us truly fulfilled if we don't learn to accept or even embrace any obstacles and difficulties this precious life has in place for us.

And most importantly: Dreaming, Hoping, and Wishing are great. Mapping out what exactly we want to happen with strategies like the Peak Performance Canvas, the DATA-Plan and the other tools I have shared in this book is excellent.

But planning alone won't let you become your best self. Manifesting those dreams and desires won't start before you actually decide to schedule your next action and then do it. Just do it. Follow your SMART MOVE and follow through. If one way towards your outcome doesn't work, try a different one immediately, and another if necessary and keep trying as long as it takes!

> "The significant problems we face cannot be solved at the same level of thinking we were at when we created them."
> — Albert Einstein

As an inventor, Thomas Edison made 1,000 unsuccessful attempts at inventing the light bulb. When a reporter asked, "How did it feel to fail 1,000 times?" Edison replied, "I didn't fail 1,000 times. The light bulb was an invention with 1,000 steps." The powerful message here is: Know your outcome, never quit and change your approach if necessary.

6 Summary and conclusion

Wrap-Up

THE JOURNEY TOWARDS ACHIEVING OUR outcomes is one that we are all on, whether we know it or not. The difference is that some people, like you the reader who has dedicated your time to read and work with this book, have a true destination. Others wonder aimlessly all the while still hoping somehow they will manage to accomplish goals or mere to-dos along the way.

Knowing your outcomes, knowing exactly WHAT you want to achieve, beautifully frames your journey: it's a powerful starting as well as finishing point. Most people who get that far immediately try to rush to the finish line, ticking all necessary to-dos off their lists.

You know there is a more effective way. You have learned that those who take a deep breath first and then follow the detour towards examining the big picture will ultimately be that much quicker, more successful and more fulfilled with their journey called life.

The foundation of this big picture lies in WHO you are and who you want to be - your identity, your core values and belief system about yourself and the world around you. WHO you are in fact is so important, that it is a barely known secret to a successful and fulfilled life. Therefore: Always start with the WHO!

You begin to understand WHY these outcomes and no others are vital for you and why you should align all your important outcomes with who you truly are.

What if you figure out that your previous goals were not supporting your nature, the real you? You have a great explanation for why those goals were doomed to fail and you can adjust them accordingly.

You have learned to not waste your vital energy on goals and action steps, which are not truly fulfilling or getting you nearer to your most important outcomes.

Once you are crystal clear on your true outcomes and understand how those support you to flourish and grow and become the person you are destined to be - you are halfway there.

The remaining steps for you to take are rather simple: the efficient execution of what you know you must achieve. After working with this book you have the most powerful tools and strategies at hand:

- How to actually set, plan and achieve your outcomes
- How to chunk them into ideal sizes
- How to formulate your SMART MOVEs to guarantee each of your goals is aligned with who you are
- How to use the DATA-Plan on a daily basis to never again get overwhelmed by too many to-dos
- How to free up energy and time from less important projects, places and people and focus all your attention towards what really matters to you

Now that you can actually visualize your specific destination and what it will feel like when you get there, you can get down to the nitty-gritty of planning the itinerary of your journey.

The science of goal setting lies in identifying the actual steps you need to take towards your journey and implementing a system that will help you execute your plans.

The art of goal achieving lies in your every-day actions. Will you decide to wonder about or pursue a concrete destination with intensity? Even if you are the grand-master of proper goal setting: Unless you maintain a positive momentum on your journey to fuel your motivation to follow through, you will get somewhere, but you won't reach that destination you want so badly to get to.

It all comes down to one important question:

What will you do today to ensure making a major step towards achieving your true outcomes?

And never forget the most important lesson you could possibly take from this book: Whatever decision you make, whatever you decide to focus on, whatever you do or stop doing: Embrace the challenges and obstacles you face as you know they are inevitable on your journey towards your very own destiny, your legacy!

Key Learnings and feed forward

> "It's not a successful climb unless you enjoy the journey."
> — Dan Benson

CONGRATULATIONS! YOU MADE IT THROUGH this book! And I'm pretty confident that you also made it through all the exercises, right? I'd sincerely like to congratulate you for this achievement. Like in this most precious game of all, you must get involved with your life; reading and working through this book is quite similar.

It is one thing to think about buying the book. The next level is, you bought it. And now what? You needed to schedule some time to go through these chapters. And working on the exercises was something that required your full attention. I presume that some passages were easy to read and understand; perhaps you are even applying some techniques for a while. Other segments were new and eventually seemed difficult and complex in the beginning.

I hope that some of my stories and ideas made you laugh and that some others made you feel stressed or were even painful. That's all great because it shows that you are engaged in the topic and that you really dare to work on yourself and strive to become your best self. For you this might sound like the most normal thing in the world, but trust me: for most people it is not!

I hope you learned a lot about yourself, new distinctions, new ideas, new insights about what is driving you and in which areas you'd like to grow further. You now also know how you are going to achieve that. And as much as I believe in the power of these proven strategies; the real change of the quality of your life only happens once you are 100% committed and start changing your habits and routines.

Never forget: It's never only about getting there! Unless of course you believe this should be the way. For most of us becoming more successful, becoming wealthier, becoming healthier, improving our relationships etc. all seem like a good idea, and for many it is. But remember that being successful without being fulfilled and feeling like you're living a meaningful life is the ultimate failure. Just think of the life the old man shared with me after my summer-bob accident.

Instead imagine: You are having tremendous fun, you are enjoying every day of the journey (=ride; =process) AND you are achieving your important goals! How would that make you feel?

In this book you have learned why this is not only very desirable but also very possible once you are living a congruent life, where your actions and habits match who you are, your core values and your belief system.

My intention was to introduce you to the WHO, WHY, WHAT and HOW of goal setting and goal achieving, which applied artfully, can massively help you to live a more meaningful, more fulfilled and more joyful life.

It is now up to you to transform any of those ideas that speak to you, to your real life. How? By just doing it right now! Put away this book, start creating your DATA Plan and pick one or two action steps in any of your important life areas. And tackle them today.

I wish you a wonderful journey, that you always know what your next SMART MOVE is and that you have the patience needed to follow through in manifesting your big dreams, desires and goals.

Enjoy the ride!

Made in the USA
Charleston, SC
10 June 2015